THE STRESS TEST

THE STRESS TEST

*How Pressure Can Make You
Stronger and Sharper*

Ian Robertson

BLOOMSBURY

NEW YORK · LONDON · OXFORD · NEW DELHI · SYDNEY

Bloomsbury USA
An imprint of Bloomsbury Publishing Plc

1385 Broadway   50 Bedford Square
New York   London
NY 10018   WC1B 3DP
USA   UK

www.bloomsbury.com

BLOOMSBURY and the Diana logo are trademarks of Bloomsbury Publishing Plc

First published in Great Britain 2016
First U.S. edition 2017

© Ian Robertson, 2016

ISBN: HB: 978-1-63286-729-2
ePub: 978-1-63286-731-5

Library of Congress Cataloging-in-Publication Data is available.

2 4 6 8 10 9 7 5 3 1

Typeset by Newgen Knowledge Works (P) Ltd., Chennai, India
Printed and bound in the U.S.A. by Berryville Graphics Inc., Berryville, Virginia

To find out more about our authors and books visit www.bloomsbury.
com. Here you will find extracts, author interviews, details of forthcoming events, and the option to sign up for our newsletters.

Bloomsbury books may be purchased for business or promotional use. For information on bulk purchases please contact Macmillan Corporate and Premium Sales Department at specialmarkets@macmillan.com.

To Geoff and Wendy, dear friends and masters of resilience.

Contents

Acknowledgements

This book would not have been written without the wise counsel and generous advice of Bill Swainson OBE, my former editor at Bloomsbury. I thank him sincerely for his painstaking professionalism, concern for accuracy and deep engagement with all his authors and their books. Nick Humphrey, my current editor at Bloomsbury, has energized me with his enthusiasm, efficiency, responsiveness and creativity and it has been a delight to work with him.

Sally Holloway of Felicity Bryan Associates is a remarkable agent who is so generous with her time and perceptive and encouraging with her advice that I cannot imagine writing a book without her support.

I have been blessed with wonderful colleagues, particularly in Dublin and in Cambridge, with whom it has been a privilege to work over the years, and I thank them all sincerely for this.

Thanks to Niall Robertson for an outstanding editorial job on the text. Deirdre and Ruairi Robertson were a source of great sense and of inspiration to me.

Dr Fiona O'Doherty, Clinical Psychologist, was my guide to the mind while I explored the brain.

I have the best family in the world and I would have achieved nothing without you.

Prologue

My fingers drummed on the desk as I waited impatiently for the computer to start up. Usually it took seconds but today it was minutes before finally the familiar screen glowed into view. I clicked on the Outlook email icon and waited . . . and waited. Finally I could access my email, but every operation was grindingly slow. The same was true for Word. My computer had gone on a go-slow, work-to-rule or whatever the digital equivalent is.

Our technician diagnosed a glitch in the software and recommended reinstalling the operating system, which she did. But no luck – the computer was still on a go-slow.

'The latest operating system is probably too big for its current RAM memory,' Lisa said. 'We need to upgrade it.'

By the next day, with new software and a bigger memory, my computer was working again and I had my digital life back.

We are used to thinking about computer performance in terms of software, hardware and their at times fraught relationship. But we have no trouble in understanding that reprogramming the software can boost hardware performance. The same, however, cannot be said for how some people, including professionals, think about the mind and the brain.

At the beginning of my career I worked for ten years as a practising clinical psychologist before moving into brain research, an unusual combination of experience that has led me to discover some crucial things about how the software of our minds and the hardware of our brains work – or don't work – together. I now realize that the mind and the brain interact with each other in ways I could never have believed when I set out on this journey.

For a long time I regarded my early work as a clinical psychologist treating people with various types of emotional problems as being unconnected with my second career as a neuroscientist looking at attention and brain rehabilitation. That made sense, because in most of science and medicine they are disconnected, too. Even nowadays, the brain's hardware researchers hardly ever talk to the mind's software practitioners, and vice versa. Gradually, however, I have come to understand that many conditions affect *both* the software and the hardware and that, just as my technician needed to deal with both of these in order to re-establish the good performance of my computer, the same is true for psychology and neuroscience.

So, belatedly, it's time for me to bring together everything I have learned from the two parts of my career. In this book I have gone back in time to review some of the cases I saw as a clinical psychologist through eyes informed by thirty years of research in neuroscience. And at the same time, I have also consciously brought my clinical psychologist's eye to bear on that hardware neuroscience research for clues as to how people can learn to cope with emotional problems and embrace the stress that follows in their wake.

It is my good fortune to have straddled the boundary between clinical psychology practice and cognitive neuroscience theory, and hence to have been able to develop a new understanding of how we can 'tune' our mind-brains, using both hardware and software, to increase our performance, to cope positively with life's adversities and to rise to challenges. That is what this book is about.

Every Monday morning, I wheeled the anaesthetized patients down to the treatment room. The psychiatrist would hold the electrodes to their heads, the bodies would judder as the current flowed, and then they would lie still. Then it was my job to wheel them back up to the ward where, an hour or two later, they would wake up, dazed and a little bewildered.

It was 1975 and I was working as a nursing assistant in a gleaming new psychiatric ward in New Zealand. Every Monday morning I had to assist in the 'treatment' – electroconvulsive therapy (ECT) – that was given to many of the patients on the ward, across many different diagnoses.

They stayed for a few weeks, very occasionally months, in this unit before they were sent on their way. Only a minority showed florid psychiatric symptoms such as hallucinations, delusions, mania or severe depression. A few were alcoholic, but the majority were suffering from depression, anxiety problems or personality disorders. I knew this because, as a graduate in psychology, I was allowed to read their notes.

Occasionally after the ECT I would witness a near-miraculous change in a profoundly depressed patient. And it was wonderful to see someone awake with a lightened spirit, having escaped from the black cave of depression. But most people seemed unchanged at best; the psychotic patients were often a little worse.

I remember one of the consultant psychiatrists who ran the unit explaining to me patiently one day that there was a clear division between mental illness, which required medical treatment, and counselling for life problems, which could be done by any reasonable person.

'The patients in here,' he told me confidently, 'are sick, and our treatments are ECT and medication – they don't need counselling.'

And so, in that ward where I worked for almost a year, everyone was on pharmaceuticals of some sort, usually several different types, and the majority were wheeled down for their ECT on a Monday morning. That was the routine.

There was, however, another consultant psychiatrist who, though nominally also responsible for the unit, very seldom admitted any of his patients to the ward, and, when he did, they were either very sick or very suicidal. Instead, he ran a day clinic where the treatment was mainly various types of psychotherapy and group therapy delivered by trained nurses and psychologists. I worked there for a few weeks as well, and it seemed to me that the types of patients being treated in the day hospital didn't differ much from those admitted to the wards by the other two doctors.

I was puzzled by the two completely different therapeutic approaches. My mentors on the ward were very clear that medical intervention of some sort was the answer to their patients' problems. However, as a psychology graduate brought up in the wake of the 1960s fashion for personal and human potential development, I was sympathetic to the approach of the third consultant – that by talking through their problems, people under great stress should be able to resolve them and so find relief from that stress.

But, if I am honest, I couldn't see a clear difference in the outcomes of the patients under the two regimes. All of which left me a bit confused.

*   *   *

It was while working as a teacher in the Fiji islands a year earlier, in 1974, that I had first come across the works of the nineteenth-century philosopher-psychologist Friedrich Nietzsche, in the sparsely furnished bookshelves of the public library in the sleepy town of Lautoka. In the absence of any more enticing reading matter I settled down to read his *Twilight of the Idols*, which, it turned out, he had written in a little under a week as an introduction to his wider work. I had studied philosophy at Glasgow University in conjunction with my psychology degree, but Nietzsche had not been part of the course.

This was a real pity as he was not only a respected philosopher, but also as influential as a psychologist in his time as Sigmund Freud. In fact, he proposed many of the ideas which are attributed to Freud, several decades before Freud did, including the concept of the unconscious and the idea that we repress uncomfortable emotions or project them on to others.[1]

At the beginning of the book Nietzsche lists forty-two separate maxims, one of which is, *What doesn't kill me, makes me stronger.*[2] He makes it clear that this isn't a new concept, quoting from the Roman poet Aulus Furius Antias 'spirits increase, vigor grows through a wound' to illustrate his point.[3] But for Nietzsche being strengthened by adversity came naturally from his belief in the existential freedom of the individual to rise above the basic drives that Freud was later to describe. In this sense and throughout his writings Nietzsche was inclined to see individuals as *agents* who could learn to harness their own power, as opposed to *subjects* of forces over which they had little control.

And so it was that I had Nietzsche at the back of my mind when I found myself among the patients in my psychiatric ward. It seemed to me that the ECT-dispensing psychiatrist who saw his patients' problems as a hardware fault couldn't have been further from Nietzsche's position – the patients, in his eyes at least, were most definitely not *agents* but the *subjects* of their emotional stress.

The psychiatrist who ran the psychotherapy ward, on the other hand, did seem to see his patients as agents in a common enterprise to find relief from stress. This made more sense to me, but nevertheless there seemed to be little difference in how the two groups of patients – hardware subjects and software agents – fared after their treatment. And for sure, neither group seemed to have become stronger through adversity. This left me confused. If people are agents of their own fears, shouldn't this mean that a course of psychotherapy would help them master life's stresses and become stronger as a result? I couldn't see much evidence of this in either ward.

So as I left the South Pacific to cross the world back to Europe, I felt split between the two perspectives and unable to reconcile them. Yes, instinctively I felt drawn to Nietzsche's belief that we can have control of the software of our minds. But when faced with the often fatalistic suffering of the patients I had worked with, I was left with the niggling doubt that maybe the first psychiatrist was right and that these patients' emotional problems could be put down to a hardware fault in the brain.

When I began my training as a clinical psychologist at the Maudsley Hospital/Institute of Psychiatry in London in October 1976 I was relieved to find that ECT was not as widely used in London hospitals as it was in New Zealand. I also learned that, soon after I had left, a new regime had been put in place in that New Zealand hospital that moderated some of the practices I had witnessed.

Most of my contemporaries at the Maudsley were students with a medical background who were training to be psychiatrists, but there were a small number, like me, who came from a psychology background and we trained in the Psychology sub-department of the Institute. The Institute's focus was on treating the 'hardware' of the brain by hunting down its faulty circuits and correcting their disordered chemistry with clever science – indeed, this is the main impetus of psychiatry to this day. And the same basic assumptions lurked in the ether of that wonderful London institution as in the New Zealand hospital – that our patients' mental problems were caused by disorders of the brain and that ultimately the brilliant, white-coated scientists hunched over their test tubes in the Institute of Psychiatry would identify the faulty biology and find cures for these conditions.

This was the background against which I trained in the Psychology Department, whose perspective was completely different from that of the psychiatrists. There I learned only to treat the 'software' without considering for a moment the hardware of the brain. Mainly, I and my fellow psychology students were taught something called 'behaviour therapy', in which people learned to overcome their phobias by gradually facing up to increasingly frightening situations. We learned to treat people with obsessive-compulsive disorders in a similar way.

But in spite of this approach of the Psychology Department, it was hard, as an impressionable student, not to get sucked into the wider Institute of Psychiatry's worldview, particularly as I found myself surrounded by so many brilliant and charismatic mentors. And there were two powerful factors in favour of it.

First was the then infant science of genetics. Within a couple of decades genetics was to achieve a remarkable flowering of scientific productivity, but during the 1970s it was dominated by twin studies, in which the balance between nature and nurture was assessed for various disorders by comparing their frequency in identical versus fraternal twins. If depression, for instance, appeared in both identical twins more often than it did in both fraternal twins, this showed that there was a strong inherited component to the depression.

Trainee psychiatrists were taught to interview patients carefully for a family history of psychiatric problems and, when evidence of such a history was found, that was usually taken as evidence of an inherited disease which could be causing the current problems.

But there was a second big reason for buying into such a medicalized view of mental problems. This was the fundamental belief – no, certainty – that the adult brain is 'hard-wired' and that, unlike a broken leg, for instance, if it is damaged it cannot repair itself.

This was the near-universal orthodoxy in medicine and neuroscience at the time, and in much of psychology, also: that experience only moulded the very young brain and that adult connections were soldered like a home electricity supply into a fixed and unchangeable neural circuitry. While houses can be rewired, brains can't, and so, from the point of view of psychiatry, we are the more or less passive servants of our genetically programmed, fixed-in-place neural circuits for the rest of our lives.

That was the belief that still clung like smoke to the curtain of assumptions underlying the world of psychiatry in which I trained and later worked. Simply put, since the brain is hard-wired, only physical or chemical treatments can change that wiring, hence the overwhelming focus on drugs and – albeit less and less often – ECT.

But while ECT was by now being used relatively rarely, the prescription of drugs for psychological disorders was expanding dramatically – and continues to do so today. Let's take one country with a centralized healthcare system and hence comprehensive records of drugs prescribed – England. In 2013, there were approximately fifty-three million people in that country.

And in that year the number of prescriptions for antidepressants was . . . fifty-three million.[4]

Even bearing in mind that many of these were repeat prescriptions, this is an astonishing rate of treatment, which does not even take into account the other types of psychotropic drugs, such as anti-anxiety medications, which are also being prescribed in enormous numbers. What is happening here? Is it the case that depression has been under-diagnosed in the past and that finally psychiatry has managed to catch up and deal with that scourge? Or are people avoiding facing up to stress for themselves, without medication, in favour of passively receiving drug treatments from their doctors? Or is it perhaps that there are more stresses these days to which people are more likely to succumb? These are huge questions to which no one, even now, seems to have clear answers.

In some ways, modern life is more stressful than it was a hundred years ago – we are faced with fragmented communities, broken families, work pressures and ruthless competition. But in many other ways life has become *less* stressful – gone are the days of the workhouse, hunger, dauntingly high levels of infant and maternal death, tuberculosis, diphtheria and the rest.

So why does there now seem to be so much more emotional distress? This was a thought that started to prey on my twenty-six-year-old mind during my encounters with the patients at the Maudsley. Many were at the extreme end of the spectrum – that's why they were there – but others had reacted badly to what I would have considered fairly unexceptional stresses in their lives and were burdened by an unhappiness that I found difficult to understand. It was also very clear to me that whatever stresses had brought them to seek treatment hadn't made them stronger.

After two years working in the world of psychiatry, I was having big doubts about Nietzsche's belief that we are the free masters of the software of our minds.

In 1982 I began working in Edinburgh, both as a practising clinical psychologist and also teaching at the university. Bringing with me what I had learned at the Maudsley, I found myself donning the mantle of the hard-nosed biologist, imparting facts to fresh-faced students such as 'the brain is not a muscle; once dead, a neuron cannot regenerate; you cannot repair damaged brains'.

My psychiatrist colleagues didn't necessarily regard their patients as brain-damaged as such, but rather that the biochemistry and wiring of their brains was askew, meaning that their brain circuits didn't work properly. This *was* potentially treatable, but only, of course, through medication or ECT. This approach to mental disorder fully accorded with the doctrine that the adult brain cannot be shaped by experience.

I passed on these orthodoxies with the grim satisfaction of the convert – all that airy-fairy 1960s optimism about personal growth and development based on self-actualization and self-improvement had to be confronted with the stark realities of the brain's physical and genetic immutability.

In 1984 I began working as a neuropsychologist in the Astley Ainslie rehabilitation hospital in Edinburgh and I continued to lecture on the theme of 'your brain is not a muscle . . .' and so on.

Until, one day, the sky fell in.

Contrary to everything I had ever been taught, a paper published in early 1984 showed that the adult brain *is not* 'hard-wired' and that, on the contrary, it *is* changed by experience.[5] Overnight, my assumptions were overturned, leading me to change the direction of my career and ultimately to convert from being a practising clinical psychologist into becoming a research neuroscientist.

The research in that paper was based on the fact that in the brains of all mammals, including humans, there are so-called 'sensory maps' in the cortex, where the brain cells' responses to sensation in different parts of the body are mapped out.

In human brains, for instance, there is a separate map for each finger, such that when one finger is touched, the sensation of being touched arises from brain cells firing on the part of the map devoted to that finger. But if that finger is lost, then the brain cells responsible for that finger quickly start responding to touch in the two neighbouring fingers. The brain, in other words, is physically changed and shaped by experience, in this case the experience of losing a finger.

The smell of orthodoxies burning filled the scientific air. Soon more research appeared showing that, if you repeatedly stimulate one fingertip, then the brain map for that fingertip expands.[6] Then it was shown that even blocking the input to the brain from one finger with a temporary anaesthetic changes the sensory maps in the brain.[7] And blind people who have learned to read Braille show an expanded brain map for the finger they use to read.[8]

A major discovery always triggers an avalanche of research, and over the next decade hundreds of papers appeared showing that an unquestioned belief for the last hundred years about the human brain was wrong: it *is* changed by experience.[9] And it isn't just the sensory/touch parts of the brain which show this plasticity – it is true for every brain system, ranging from hearing[10] to language[11] to attention[12] to memory.[13]

Crucially for my own bewildered journey through Nietzschean optimism and genetic fatalism, it transpired that our emotional experiences also physically shape our brains.

Take babies, for example. Through the work of John Bowlby, in particular, it has been well known for a long time that it is important for newborn babies to form strong, emotionally secure relationships with their mothers. However, for some unlucky children that doesn't happen. Children with so-called 'insecure attachment', whose mothers tend to be less responsive to their emotional needs, suffer more anxiety and are less easily soothed when distressed than securely attached children. And the effects of this are very long lasting.

When secure and insecure eighteen-month-old babies were followed up when they were twenty-two years old, those young people who had been insecurely attached as babies, and hence who had suffered a lot of anxiety in their lives, showed important differences in the amygdala, a key part of the brain responsible for emotion. The amygdala is particularly active when people are anxious, and so, over many years, this leads to it becoming bigger because its networks of brain cells become more and more strongly connected with repeated use. And, indeed, the twenty-two-year-olds whose relationships with their mothers had been insecure, even though they would not be termed mentally ill, had bigger amygdalae than those with secure relationships.[14]

I was dizzied by this discovery: the software of experience can re-engineer the hardware of the brain.

I began to feel the way I imagine Nietzsche must have felt a century earlier when he saw his religious idols fall. Mine was a different idol: the brain disease theory of emotional distress. And the first of its orthodoxies – that the adult brain is hard-wired – had been tilted so badly that the idol was in danger of falling off its pedestal. But it was still standing because of the second stark, biological reality holding upright my idol of a medical view of emotional disorders: genetics.

We have roughly 24,000 genes and they don't change with experience – we are, more or less, stuck with what we inherit. The notion of the hard-wired brain may have fallen, but my idol was still standing because of this brute fact about our inherited make-up. My psychiatric colleagues' focus on family history in their patient assessments made clear sense in the light of this biological reality, as did the worldwide effort to find medical solutions to what appeared to be strongly genetically determined emotional illnesses such as depression, obsessive-compulsive disorders and chronic anxiety problems. Because the twin studies were clear – there was a strong inherited element to most emotional disorders.

And then, with a crash, the idol suddenly fell to the ground.

It was 1990 and research appeared telling me something about genes that I knew but hadn't properly understood before: while their basic structure can't be changed by external events, the way they work *can* be changed.[15] Genes work by 'expressing' proteins and these proteins then control various functions in our bodies, brains and behaviour. Experiences and environment can turn on and turn off genes' protein-synthesizing activity.[16, 17, 18] This is true of one particular experience common to every one of my patients in New Zealand, London and Edinburgh. And that experience is *stress*.

Exams are stressful for most people, which is why researchers in Ohio studied the activity of a gene called the interleukin-2 receptor in medical students during exam periods as compared with non-stressful times when they had no exams. The researchers discovered that stress turned down the activity of this gene,[19] which is central to the working of the body's immune system.

Many later studies found similar effects of stress on gene function. For instance, London civil servants who felt stressed by having to do mental tasks under time pressure showed big changes in the functioning of another immune system gene that contributes to the hardening of the arteries (atherosclerosis). The interleukin-1 beta gene 'expresses' a protein that plays a key part in inflammation. The men most stressed by the tasks showed the biggest increase in this gene's activity, with the effects lasting two hours or more after it had ended.[20]

The final collapse of my idol confirmed me in my decision to become a researcher and to try to understand this incredible interaction between the software of the mind and the hardware of the brain.

As the last decade of the twentieth century began, I realized that it didn't make sense to think of mind and brain as separate software and hardware entities – we had to consider how they interact and affect each other. Thoughts and emotions turn genes on and off, physically reshaping the brain as they do so. And then these physical changes in turn mould our thoughts and emotions.

It made no sense to search for the physical causes of emotional distress independently of the psychological stressors creating the turmoil. Nor did it make any sense for psychologists to give no thought to the hardware of the brain when delivering their psychological therapies. The absurdity of separating mind and brain – a view that had surrounded me in New Zealand, London and Edinburgh – hit me like a brick and set me on a new career in neuroscience research.

But one doubt still kept circulating in my mind that was a remnant of my old hardware-fixated self: if psychological stressors can physically change the brain, including gene function, surely psychological therapies should be able to do the same? I had to wait another twenty years before that doubt was resolved. Talking and behaviour therapies *can* physically change the brain: for instance, successful cognitive behaviour therapy

(CBT) for obsessive-compulsive disorders can lead to significant changes in brain function, one of the early such studies discovered.[21] Many others were to follow which showed that changes to the software of the mind can actually cause changes to the brain's hardware.[22]

Would my New Zealand psychiatrist, convinced that only physical therapies such as ECT could cure what he saw as the brain's hardware faults, have had more respect for his psychotherapy delivering consultant colleague had he known this fact? And would that software-focused consultant have taken a different approach to his psychotherapy had *he* known that stress had altered the hardware of his patients' brains? I believe that the answer to both these questions is 'yes'.

I felt liberated to be caught on this revolutionary scientific wave, which swept me to Rome in 1989 for a year of research into brain plasticity. By now I was convinced that Nietzsche had at least the theoretical possibility of being right – what we do with our minds has consequences for our brains and vice versa. Stress *does* have the potential to make you stronger in terms of both your software *and* your hardware. Now the challenge for me was to find out how to put this principle into practice, and that is what I have been trying to do for the three decades since.

In 1991, I had the great fortune to get a job at the Applied Psychology Unit in Cambridge, since renamed the Cognition and Brain Sciences Unit. There I took forward my ideas on how we can best use our knowledge about how the software and hardware of the brain interact, to help people improve their performance and rise to the challenges facing them.

In 1999, I wrote a book called *Mind Sculpture* about this scientific revolution,[23] and moved to Trinity College Dublin, convinced more than ever that Nietzsche was on to something, but wanting to understand the concept from a more scientific perspective.

The human brain is the most complex entity in the known universe and Nietzsche's maxim recognizes in a philosophical sense the human ability to harness some of that complexity in shaping our own destiny. Only when we give up our idols, Nietzsche argues, can mankind reach its potential, by using its own willpower to forge its destiny.

During my time as a clinical psychologist, I tried to address my patients' individual symptoms as best I could, but, I now realized, the assumption of the fixed-in-place brain circuitry had infiltrated my thinking and, as a result, sapped my confidence in my own ability to achieve with those early patients. And my own fatalism may even have communicated itself subtly to some of them, tethering them to the false idol of the unchangeable brain and thus disabling their inherent capacity shared by every living human being to have a hand in shaping their own neural destiny.

The big idea that now started brewing in my mind was trying to understand the interactions of the mind and the brain in order to help explain why some people are crushed by the problems life throws at them while others seem toughened by them. As I moved to Dublin, and into the twenty-first century, I was convinced that only by combining what we know about the hardware and the software of the brain, as well as how they interact, could we really explore the limits of Nietzsche's maxim. How, when and why do some people rise to the challenge of bad experiences, while others fold under their weight?

This book draws on my own and other people's research but also on my first-hand observations of cases when I worked as a clinical psychologist. I have gone back to my old cases with new eyes and tried to understand them in the light of hundreds of research studies that have only emerged in the last decade and which have revolutionized our understanding of the mind, the brain and our emotions. My reminiscences are tinged with irrational regret, because I now believe that, had I known then what I now know, I could have offered so much more to these people.

My consolation, however, is that I can offer the discoveries I have made, and the practical advice that people reading this book can take from them, to a much wider audience. I have no doubt that everyone can learn to better control their own mind and emotions and, if they do so, they can within limits turn stress to their own advantage. The main purpose of this book is to explain how and why this is possible through a better understanding of how the software and hardware interact with each other.

Two cases from my Edinburgh days come to mind which exemplify the difference between how different people react to stress in very different ways. I have disguised all the individuals described in this book by changing their names, key details of their lives, as well as jobs and locations.

Lucy had been sent to me by her tutor. Twenty, tall, blonde, her good looks were marred only by the dark smudges under tired eyes, and a downcast, nervy appearance. Sitting on the edge of her chair, this well-dressed, well-spoken but tearful young woman from a privileged background twisted the damp tissue in her hands as she tried to explain what was wrong. She hadn't been sleeping properly for months, she told me, and had been losing weight because her appetite had disappeared. Her social life at university had dwindled to an occasional drink with a close friend and she had been missing lectures because she felt so exhausted in the morning following her sleepless nights.

After nearly two hours of talking to Lucy, I discovered that these problems had emerged, more or less out of the blue, six months earlier. Before that, she had been healthy and happy for her entire life. So what had happened six months previously?

I kept checking again and again that there wasn't something more to it, but no. Here was the cause of Lucy's anxiety: she had, for the first time in her life, failed an exam, and a non-critical mid-year exam at that. No matter that she had passed it second time round, this 'failure' had floored her, psychologically speaking. Her reaction to such a relatively minor setback couldn't have been further from 'what doesn't kill me, makes me stronger' – it was more like 'what hurts me slightly has caused me psychological near-collapse'. And I kept coming across people like Lucy in my early years as a clinical psychologist whose experiences matched hers.

But then there were other cases that seemed to vindicate the philosopher's insight. Another student at the university was sent to see me at the insistence of his tutor. He came reluctantly. Like Lucy, Peter had been missing lectures – but for a quite different reason. Peter's mother had died of cancer at roughly the same time that Lucy had failed her mid-year exam. His father, who had lost his job because of the time he had taken off to care for his wife, had not coped well with her death and was drinking heavily. Financially, things were very tough and Peter had had to step in to protect his fourteen-year-old sister as much as possible from the misfortunes that had hit the family.

The tutor had been concerned that Peter might himself be suffering psychologically and that this was the reason for his non-attendance at some lectures. But it turned out that there was a much more prosaic reason for his absence. Peter had taken on a part-time job to help the family.

And there was nothing wrong with Peter mentally speaking, either. On the contrary, the misfortune 'has turned me round', he told me. Before his mother became sick, he had been a heavy drinking, good-time fresher who, though turning up to most of his lectures, just scraped through his exams and assignments. He didn't have any real interest in his studies and gave little thought to the future. Now this had all changed. He was focused and studying hard, making up for lost lectures in the evening after he finished his job. He had decided he wanted to study medicine and was planning to take the exams which would allow him to transfer to that subject.

Peter did admit to feeling stressed at times, but there was a glint in his eye as he described how he coped with the big demands being made on him. What hadn't killed Peter had certainly strengthened him.

So what *was* it about Peter that made him respond to stress in the way he did? And why did Lucy succumb to it the way *she* did?

After more than three decades of research, I now understand why Nietzsche's maxim applied to Peter but not to Lucy. Like my slowed-down computer, both faced problems because of stress. But Peter managed to patch his software on his own by reprogramming his approach to life from one of directionless drifting to that of a highly focused motivation to care for his family and train as a doctor. This software fix, as I was to discover much later, was helped by the resulting boost in the hardware performance of his brain.

Lucy, however, needed my help to fix the software glitch of her exaggerated reaction to an exam failure. One reason she couldn't sort it out for herself was that her particular psychological reaction had adversely affected the hardware of her brain. Rather than boosting its performance, as in Peter's case, it had depressed its functioning, so making it much harder for her to reprogram her brain's software herself.

I have discovered that you can explain the different reactions of Peter and Lucy to stress by studying how the software of their minds interacts with the hardware of their brains.

And to describe how *that* happens, I have to tell you the story of how I discovered the existence of the brain's tipping point.

Why Do Engineers Build Bends in Roads?

Civil engineers build bends in roads on flat, empty plains, spending hundreds of millions of dollars on these costly, physically unnecessary curves. This strange practice means that long, straight roads are not very common. If you are keen to search one out, you might like to go to the Eyre Highway in Australia, which runs like an arrow for ninety-one miles, or, in the USA, North Dakota's Highway 46, which tracks almost ruler-straight for 123 miles. But driving along them is a disorienting and difficult experience* and long roads like these spawn many single-vehicle accidents when people simply drive off them. Why is this? What could be easier than keeping the car going straight without having to put any effort into turning, judging curves or slowing down for them?

I never gave a thought to bends in roads until two people I knew were killed in two separate train crashes.

On 8 August 1996, my colleague Ruth Holland left her office at the *British Medical Journal* in London and walked the short distance to Euston station, where she boarded the 17.04 to Milton Keynes. Twenty minutes later, the driver of the train

---

* See this YouTube video of just a tiny stretch of the Eyre Highway
http://www.youtube.com/watch?v=7wvCUjnwyrQ

passed through a red light and crashed into another train at Watford South Junction, killing Ruth and injuring 69 others.

When the report on the accident came out, the enquiry concluded that the driver of Ruth's train had passed through two yellow warning lights without reacting, before crossing the final, red light. Upset at the loss of a dear colleague, I decided to find out what had gone so wrong that the train driver did not do something as simple as slow to a warning light. It so happened that this personal interest fed into a scientific and medical problem I was wrestling with at the time at the Applied Psychology Unit in Cambridge.

We were trying to find ways of helping people with brain damage regain cognitive function. John was a film cameraman who had fallen from a moving truck on a set, hitting his head and suffering brain damage. John was exceptionally smart and, as I sat giving him test after test, he got top scores on almost all of them, showing great focus, good memory and a high ability to solve problems. I couldn't find any real evidence of abnormality. So, what was the problem, you might ask? Here are extracts from our conversation when I met him and his wife. Their three-year-old, Andrew, was playing outside, being minded by one of our students while John's wife held a baby in her arms.

'John, are you having any particular problems since your accident?'

'I lost my job – I don't know what to do with myself half the time.'

'Do you notice any problems with your memory or concentration?'

'No, not really . . . Jane keeps saying I'm scatty . . .' He glances over at his wife who sits, looking very tense in the corner.

'You've noticed changes, Jane?' I ventured.

'John, how can you say that you don't have any problems!' she snapped. 'I left you minding Andrew for just an hour yesterday and when I came back, he was on his own.' Her voice was trembling.

'I just rode my bike down the road to test the new tyres,' he muttered, 'I would have been back soon.'

'Don't lie!' she hissed. 'I saw the expression on your face when you came back – you had completely forgotten about Andrew! Imagine if I had left you with the baby . . . !' At that, Jane burst into tears.

John's life was in chaos. Jane was threatening to leave him and he could no longer work as a cameraman because he was so unreliable. All this was because he had turned into an extreme scatterbrain: in everyday life there was little sign of the intelligent, cognitively well-functioning person I saw across the desk from me. He was careless, thoughtless and unreliable enough to forget he was looking after his young child.

The contradiction between the smart John of my tests and the scatterbrain sitting before me niggled at me. But when Ruth Holland died in that train accident, an idea began to spark somewhere in my mind. Was there some connection between a train driver's fatal mistake and John's chaotic inability to carry out the basic routines of everyday life? Maybe there is something about routine, I thought, which somehow 'switches off' those smart abilities that I knew both John and the train driver had.

So I gave John some very simple tests that were meant to simulate the dull routine of the train driver's cabin. I programmed the computer to flash up numbers between 1 and 9 randomly. John simply had to keep watching the screen, and then press the space bar when he saw a 3. It was a boring task – just like driving a train – and, to my disappointment,

John did just fine. Even for a mind-numbing half hour and over a thousand numbers, with each 3 appearing randomly on average every 9 numbers, John hardly missed any: as far as yet another test was concerned, John was doing well. But I *knew* that in real life he wasn't.

I tried many other similar types of tests, attempting to recreate the conditions of everyday routine, but still John did well on all of them. Was I running up against the limits of neuropsychology? We were supposed to be able to use sophisticated, standard tests to measure mental abilities, but here I was being mocked by a set of problems that John's wife, and even young children, could see clearly, but which I could not show up in my tests – and hence could not understand.

Thank goodness for teatime in Cambridge. The Medical Research Council's Applied Psychology Unit (now the Cognition and Brain Sciences Unit), where I had worked since 1991, is a remarkable place with one iron-clad rule: come out of your office or lab for tea overlooking the croquet lawn at 10.30 sharp in the morning and at four in the afternoon – and talk science. So one morning, after months of failing to work out what was going wrong with John, I happened to be sitting beside my colleague Jackie Andrade, bemoaning my failures.

I explained how I knew there was something wrong with John but that no tests I had been able to devise so far could show it. I said that it didn't seem to be a problem with keeping his mind focused in boring situations because he could press a button when he saw a 3 or any other target indefinitely. Tea finished, I went back to my office. Half an hour later, Jackie called me up to her lab.

'Try this,' she said.

I looked and there was my simple test, with numbers randomly flashing between 1 and 9.

'I've tried that already,' I replied glumly.

'No you haven't – press to every number *except* the three,' she smiled.

Sceptically, I began pressing the space bar for each number except 3.

'Damn!'

I had pressed the fourth 3 by accident, so I kept going.

'Whoa! – not again – I wasn't paying attention!' I pressed another 3. 'Jackie, what's going on here? Why do I keep pressing some of the threes?'

Jackie was laughing. She had also been doing the test and had made fewer mistakes than I had, but had still found it hard to resist hitting the 3s. So had I been using my test in the wrong way? It seems that I might have been.

I couldn't wait to try Jackie's version of the test on John. I felt bad celebrating someone's difficulties but, yes! – he was much worse than I was. He kept pressing many of the 3s, even though he knew he shouldn't. A polite lad, again and again he muttered 'Oops!' – so often that that became the title of the paper based on our work with him which we published in 1997, a year after Ruth Holland's death.[1] This test – which we called the SART (Sustained Attention to Response Test) – is now used across the world to assess the effects of a whole raft of medical conditions, from chronic insomnia to depression and Alzheimer's disease.

I gradually worked out what was happening: tapping the space bar whenever the 3 appeared is relatively easy for the brain because it can quickly put it under 'automatic pilot' control. This happens when, as the brain becomes more used to a new task, it gradually moves control of it from its higher cortical regions to subcortical areas called the basal ganglia and the cerebellum. These parts of the brain can then 'run off' the newly mastered routine without involving the cortex. This is why, once you've learned to, you don't forget how to ride a bike.

The trick of the 'don't press to 3' SART that made it so hard for John was that he had to *switch off* this automatic pilot when the 3 appeared. This 'inhibition' of the automatic pilot is itself very hard to make automatic and so needs you to stay alert and mentally focused. And in a boring task like this, that is difficult for anyone, but especially so for John.

The SART puts the habit and the conscious control parts of the brain in conflict with each other. The conscious control parts of the brain have to keep checking what the automatic pilot is up to and from time to time switch it off, or 'inhibit' it. I discovered a few years later, with the help of then newly developed brain imaging methods, that this inhibition takes place in the frontal lobes of the brain.[2]

The simple switch in the new test from remembering to press to remembering *not* to press actually captured much better than any of my other tests what our lives are usually like. Most of what we do – get up, shower, have breakfast, etc. – is automatic and routine. And for a very good reason – imagine how exhausting it would be to have to plan and think about these things every time we do them.

But sometimes these automatic pilot routines get us into trouble. For instance, recently my smartphone memory was full, so I set about deleting some of the photographs from it. I swiped pressed delete, swiped pressed delete, swiped pressed delete . . . and so on. Within just ten to twenty seconds my brain had helpfully put this set of movements into automatic pilot and . . . damn! I deleted a photograph I wanted to keep. Even though I had told myself to make sure to keep that photo when I started the delete-fest, my cerebellum took control of my fingers, making them press delete while my inattentive frontal lobes were distracted by something less repetitive and more interesting.

So one of the secrets of getting through the day without too many hitches is to be able to stop routines at the right time and not get carried along under the control of the automatic pilot parts of the brain. This is called *inhibition* and to know *when* to inhibit you have to monitor yourself and your actions. In particular, this is what you have to do when driving a train.

It appears that one of the hardest things for the human brain to do is to keep alert and focused during such routine and the ability to do so is called 'sustained attention'. As I went about trying to find the reasons for Ruth Holland's death, I discovered that lapses in this sustained attention are the single biggest cause of railway accidents in the world.[3]

I also discovered something else which surprised me: several laboratories across the world were using SART – to study depression. I hadn't known this at the time because my research was focused on people with brain damage, but it turns out that our ability to cope with stress is closely linked with the type of sustained attention that SART measures, as you will see in the next chapter.

So finally I had managed to capture in the lab the sorts of problems John's family was facing. Now I could begin to work out what exactly was going on in his brain and, more importantly, find out how to help him get back to work and, if possible, save his marriage. However, something was still not right. OK, I had shown that John found it tough to sustain his attention, but surely this poor concentration should have caused problems in the tests I had given him before – but he did just fine in those.

Many tea breaks at the Applied Psychology Unit went by without my solving this second problem. Then the 2002 Nobel Prizes were announced. To my delight, they gave the prize for economics to a psychologist, Daniel Kahneman – a former colleague who had been at Oxford University before moving to Princeton, where his work on human happiness had forced economists to revise their assumptions about the rational basis for human economic choices.

This prompted me to reconsider Kahneman's work. While in Oxford, the Nobel Laureate's research had been not on happiness but, rather, on attention and I had read his book *Attention and Effort* several years before. With a half-conscious inkling about a possible solution to the John conundrum, I hurried to the library and picked out Kahneman's slim and somewhat dusty volume. (This book has twice proved to be critical to my own research. Once with John, and then again more than a decade later when a rereading of it helped me to an understanding of one of the biggest issues surrounding Alzheimer's disease – but I'll come back to that in Chapter 5.)

Strangely enough, the book focused on the pupil of the eye. When you see someone that you like, your pupils dilate – and the same thing happens when you get a fright. But Kahneman discovered that other, less emotional things also make your pupils dilate. When he gave people arithmetic problems, he noticed that their pupils grew bigger. Not only that but *any mental challenge* dilated them. For instance, picking out a sound that differed only very slightly in pitch from other distracting sounds had the same effect on the pupil. What's more, he discovered that the harder the challenge the more the pupil dilated, and also that this opening of the pupil to challenge was an automatic response. Being taxed mentally seemed to trigger something in the brain, and the dilated pupil was a signal of that brain change. It would be ten years before I discovered what that change was.

My own pupils must have dilated as I read this. I now realized why John did so well in my tests but so badly at home: *challenge*. When John sat down at the desk to do my tests, they were difficult, and his brain responded accordingly. I didn't measure his pupil dilation, but my bet is that they would have got bigger in response to this challenge, just as Nobel Prize winner Daniel Kahneman had shown.

In the routine of everyday life, such as minding his children or organizing family life, the true challenges may have been great, but to John's brain they seemed routine and boring, and so did not 'switch on' whatever this extra crucial brain process was. It was this mystery process that made him do so well on all my neuropsychological tests . . . except SART. Something about *difficulty* nudged John into performing better and Jackie's version of the SART, which had appeared so deceptively easy to me, showed up his problems as none of my other tests did. I felt that I was at last getting closer to understanding John. And then the second rail accident occurred.

On 28 February 2001, an old colleague of mine, the psychologist Steve Baldwin, boarded the early morning train at York on his way to a meeting in London. At 6.13 a.m., a Land Rover plunged off a neighbouring motorway, landing on the track in front of Steve's train, which hit it, sending it into the path of an approaching coal train, killing Steve and nine others. The car driver was jailed for five years because he had fallen asleep at the wheel, having spent the previous night on an internet chat room.

The shock of Steve's death made me think some more about Ruth Holland's accident and about my ideas on what was wrong with John. Could it be that the 'something' behind these problems was simply a kind of sleepiness? My colleagues and I at the Applied Psychology Unit quickly decided to test this idea with the help of a willing and sleep-resistant medical student intern.

He managed to persuade ten of his fellow students at Peterhouse College in Cambridge to let him bring his computer to their rooms and carry out our SART four times a day for four days – at 7 a.m., 1 p.m., 7 p.m. and 1 a.m. – having agreed to make sure they were awake before he arrived. The results confirmed our suspicions: when they were at their sleepiest, at 7 a.m. and 1 a.m., the students pressed the 3 much more often than during the day. We called the resulting scientific paper 'Coffee in the cornflakes'.[4] It certainly helped the student understand how easy it is for sleepy doctors to make occasionally fatal mistakes in the middle of the night, such as working out drug dosages wrongly or forgetting to turn on drips.

These were exactly the sorts of absent-minded mistakes that John made, raising the question of whether some sort of 'sleepiness' leading to SART errors by the Cambridge students late at night, lay behind John's problems of inattentiveness in his life.

So, was John just a bad sleeper? Did my two colleagues die because of two drowsy drivers? Is good sustained attention simply a matter of being fully awake? Well, it so happens that John, like many brain-injured people, was indeed a bad sleeper. And certainly Steve Baldwin died because a car driver fell asleep at the wheel, although it was less clear cut in the case of Ruth Holland's train driver. So I pondered again how drowsiness and attention may be linked and decided to refresh my hazy memories of what I had studied about sleep and the brain.

The Cambridge students were drowsy at 1 a.m. and at 7 a.m., I remembered, because their brains' night–day sleep–wake clock was ticking deep in their brain in a spot called the 'supra-chiasmatic nucleus' (SCN). This timekeeper acts as a kind of switch in our brains which, with the help of inhibitor chemical messengers, turns down the simmering activity of our cortex to help make us sleepy at night. It then does the reverse in the morning, kicking our brain into gear by lifting the night-time inhibition. This is critical for our health and for our memory, as a good night's sleep is one of the many things that help us bind new memories into our brains. But how might this explain the students' mistakes on the SART? Was there any clue about how drowsiness and attention might interact?

And then, with extraordinarily good timing, a paper was published by Gary Aston-Jones and his colleagues at Princeton University. It showed for the first time that the sleep timekeeper was connected up to one of the brain's key attention centres, known as the 'locus coeruleus'.[5] This tiny cluster of cells deep in the stem of the brain is virtually the only source of one of the brain's key chemical messengers, *noradrenaline*, or, as it is known in the USA, *norepinephrine*. It is one of a handful of messengers which helps us to pay attention. Aston-Jones discovered that when we notice something new, or surprising, or potentially rewarding, or indeed frightening, the locus coeruleus (usually referred to as the LC) spreads noradrenaline to almost every part of the brain, reaching them all in a few hundred thousandths of a second, far more extensively than other chemical messengers such as dopamine.[6]

So when the sleep–wake controller, the suprachiasmatic nucleus, starts to close down the daytime functions to prepare for sleep, part of its purpose is to quieten this LC puppy dog that gets so easily excited by new thoughts, surprising ideas, interest-ing patterns on the wall and so on. It switches down the LC activity and that of some other arousal centres in the brain so that we can drift off to sleep undisturbed by excitements, novelties or fearful thoughts.

And as we sleepily emerge from night's oblivion, our LC begins to fire up again as the SCN releases its hold on it. Along with some other centres in the brain, it turns the tables on the SCN and *inhibits* it. Maybe with the additional help of a cup of coffee, the LC's growing activity clamps down on the sleep controller and wakes you up.[7]

Drowsiness and attention are like rivals for control over our consciousness. Drowsiness has a slow day–night cycle usually referred to as the 'circadian rhythm'. The timing of this rhythm varies from one individual to another and also changes as we get older. While adolescents and young adults are notoriously prone to going to bed late and waking up late, older people – and indeed older animals – tend to move their cycle so that they wake early and also go to sleep earlier than when they were young.

It's harder to focus and avoid pouring coffee into our cornflakes at 4 a.m. than it is at 11 a.m. because at 4 a.m. the SCN sleep controller is in charge, inhibiting the LC. Trying to solve problems or study late at night can be difficult because the LC doesn't offer the amount of noradrenaline your brain needs for concentration and learning.

But even in the early evening, well into your alert time as far as the SCN is concerned, focus is not guaranteed. Remember that the LC and the SCN are at loggerheads, each trying to switch off the other. If for whatever reason the LC's activity goes down, the suprachiasmatic nucleus is waiting, ever ready, to sneak its beloved cloak of sleep over the brain. And what sort of thing might reduce the LC's friskiness? A tedious lecture, a bad movie or a monotonous raconteur will do the trick, as will, of course . . . a highway without bends.

So that is why engineers spend so much money building apparently pointless bends into roads: to rescue the locus coeruleus from its bullying rival, the SCN sleep controller. Just as a boring lecturer can lull an otherwise alert audience into slumber, and an exciting speaker can keep awake a class of sleep-starved students, so a simple bend in the highway can present a sufficiently novel, modest challenge to make the LC inject sleep-inhibiting noradrenaline into the brain.

Steve Baldwin died because, in the brain of the driver of the Land Rover that derailed his train, the locus coeruleus lost its struggle with the suprachiasmatic nucleus. He could not stay alert that morning because he had so weighted the battle in his brain in favour of the SCN by taking very little sleep the night before. This was the same sort of circadian rhythm sleepiness that reduced students' 1 a.m. SART performance and that was also the source of John's problems.

I knew that low noradrenaline levels cause sleepiness. So, I began to wonder – could this lack of a crucial chemical messenger in the brain explain John's problem, too? But there was a problem – I had no way of measuring noradrenaline in the brain, and so couldn't test this hypothesis. I was stuck.

By this time I had moved to Trinity College Dublin where one of my colleagues, Michael Gill, was studying the genetics of ADHD – Attention Deficit Hyperactivity Disorder. ADHD can be caused by a number of factors. However, I discovered in a chance conversation with Michael that there was a form of a gene that, if a child inherited one or two copies of it from their mother, father or both, they were somewhat more likely to have ADHD than a child without it. What made me very excited was that this form of the gene – the so-called "T allele of the DBH c-1021T polymorphism" (dopamine beta-hydroxylase), affected how much noradrenaline was available to the brain.

Here at last I had an opportunity to see whether the clue offered by Steve Baldwin's untimely death was borne out: were the LC and noradrenaline involved in the sorts of attention problems that John showed? If I was right, then ADHD children who had one or two copies of the gene that left their brains short of noradrenaline should do worse on the SART test than ADHD children *without* the risky form of the gene.

We managed to get a grant to answer this question and employed a talented Australian postdoc called Mark Bellgrove to address it. It took two years of Mark driving around the back roads of Ireland, testing children diagnosed with ADHD, to come up with the answer. It had been a risky prediction: all the children had ADHD, with similar symptoms of poor concentration and impulsivity. We were forecasting that the SART test would tell apart from among these indistinguishable children, those with and without the form of the gene which influenced how much noradrenaline they had in their brains.

I gave a whoop of joy when the results came through. Not only did the SART test distinguish children with and without the risky form of the DBH gene, but the errors in the SART were greater for those with two copies than those with one, and both made many more errors than the ADHD children who had no copies of it.[8] Finally I was beginning to find the links between attention, challenge and the chemistry of the brain – crucial ingredients in the recipe for good attention.

But, as always in science, doubt began to niggle me. I had only shown this in a particular group of children with ADHD. If attention and noradrenaline actually were involved in bends in the highway, scatterbrain fathers and accident-prone drivers, then I should be able to see this link at work in ordinary, healthy adults as well. I set Ciara Greene, one of my Trinity PhD students, the task of testing a group of Dubliners who had either zero, one or two copies of the risky form of the gene that affected how much noradrenaline was available to their brains.

Ciara's results confirmed my theory. In ordinary, healthy adults, those whose genetic make-up gave their brains slightly less noradrenaline were more likely than the others to make the 'Oops!' response and press the number 3 on the SART.[9] So this didn't just apply to ADHD, I was glad to see.

It is very easy for scientists to get excited about small, abstract things and for non-scientists to scratch their heads and wonder about the relevance of such academic concerns apparently so far from real life. The clinical psychologist in me wanted to know whether pressing the space bar in response to the number 3 actually mattered at all, noradrenaline or no noradrenaline. My fellow clinical psychologist Tom Manly was more than happy to help find out.

Tom and I gathered together two groups of ordinary, healthy adults who differed in only one respect – how absent-minded they were. The great psychologist Donald Broadbent, who had been a colleague of Nobel Prize winner Daniel Kahneman at Oxford, had devised a way of measuring how prone individuals were to absent-mindedness through what they called the 'Cognitive Failures Questionnaire'. Below are the types of questions he asked – the more these apply to you, the more absent-minded you are in everyday life. Answer 'very often', 'quite often', 'occasionally', 'very rarely' or 'never' to each, giving 1 point for 'never' and 5 points for 'very often'.

- Do you read something, realize you haven't been taking it in, so you have to read it again?
- Do you find you forget why you went from one part of the house to another?
- Do you find that you miss signposts you are looking for while driving?

- When giving directions, do you mix up left and right?
- Are you inclined to bump into people?
- Do you have to go back to check whether you have turned off a light or cooker, or locked the door?
- Do you find you haven't been listening to people's names when you are introduced to them?
- Do you say something and only afterwards realize that it might have been taken as insulting?
- When you are occupied with something, do you fail to hear someone speaking to you?
- Do you lose your temper and regret it afterwards?
- Do you leave important emails, messages or letters unanswered for days?
- When on a road you know well but don't use often, do you forget which way to turn?
- When looking for something in the supermarket do you find that it has been in front of your eyes the whole time?
- Do you find yourself wondering out of the blue whether you have used a word correctly?
- Is making up your mind a problem for you?
- Do you forget appointments?
- Do you find that you have forgotten where you have laid something down, like keys or spectacles?
- Do you find you accidentally throw away the thing you wanted to keep and keep the thing you wanted to throw away?
- Does your mind wander when you should be listening?
- Do you forget people's names?
- Do you start doing one thing and then accidentally get distracted into doing another?
- Do you find that something is 'on the tip of your tongue' but you can't quite remember it?
- Do you forget what you came to the shops to buy?

- Do you tend to drop things?
- Do you find that you can't think of anything to say?

The maximum score you can get on this questionnaire is 125 – though we never saw anyone who said 'very often' (5 points) to every one of the twenty-five questions. Absent-mindedness is a continuum but the average adult scores around 40–60 on the test.

We had already found that people with brain injuries like cameraman John showed these types of problems. But they, like John, weren't particularly aware of their own scatterbrain behaviour. Later, we discovered that lack of self-awareness is closely linked to this type of inattention, which I'll come back to in Chapter 4.

John's family endured John's absent-mindedness day in and day out, and so did the families of our other brain-injured participants. What's more, the worse they did on the SART, the more absent-minded their families said they were. So my inner clinical psychologist was reassured that the SART wasn't just some irrelevant computer test unrelated to everyday life: far from it, it was quite a good predictor of brain-injured people's day-to-day difficulties.

But is this test relevant to you and me, who haven't suffered brain injury, or to the ordinary train driver who fatally lost concentration? Tom and I gave the SART to ordinary people, who were either high or low on everyday cognitive failures – and, sure enough, the more absent-minded people made twice as many mistakes on the SART as the low scorers.[10] Then, I was delighted to see, some independent Canadian researchers found the same.[11]

But, as always in science, you have to keep looking for better evidence. Could it be, I wondered, that despite being of roughly equal intelligence, the absent-minded group were just generally less good at paying attention than the other group? Maybe there was nothing specific to sustained attention about this noradrenaline-sensitive SART?

To try this out, we programmed a test very similar to the SART, but one in which every second number was, on average, a 3. Doing this feels very different from the normal SART, where the 3s come unpredictably around 10 per cent of the time. In this new 50 per cent version of the test, the 3s keep coming unpredictably but very often, and there is little chance of the participant being lulled into the rhythm of routinely pressing to all the other numbers.[12]

Exactly as we predicted, the absent-minded people flourished on this test – performing as well as other people – as did John. Why so? Again, *challenge*. The 3s coming fast and furious switched on something in John's brain that was missing in his everyday life, and also to a lesser extent in scatterbrained ordinary people. Civil engineers had figured out that this something was needed when they designed bends into highways, simply from looking at the accident statistics.

Our 50 per cent 3s test was the equivalent of a very twisty, bendy road, where you have no choice but to stay alert and focused because of the challenge. John and our absent-minded volunteers had no problem in that sort of situation; they *did* have problems when the external challenge was missing and so had to supply that missing 'something' from inside their own heads.

Our theory that John's problems were partly a result of a lack of noradrenaline now had a lot of evidence behind it from our studies of people with ADHD. But I still had a problem: where precisely 'inside their heads' was this supposed control centre that ensured a sufficient supply of that missing 'something'? We knew that this sort of attention was closely linked to noradrenaline in the brain, but which parts of the brain were involved in supplying the mental equivalent of the bend in the road? To cut a long story short, I carried out one brain-imaging study on the SART with Tom Manly and colleagues at Cambridge[13] and another with Brian Levine at the Rotman Institute in Toronto[14] – and both came up with the same result.

The right outside surface of the front of the brain, the so-called 'dorsolateral prefrontal cortex' – roughly corresponding to the brain surface lying below your right temple – was critically involved in supplying mental bends in the road by triggering the release of noradrenaline in the brain. This was a very significant discovery, because it turned out that this same part of the brain was involved in something even more interesting than sustained attention: self-awareness, which, I was to find out years later, is a crucial ingredient in coping positively with stress.

But what were we going to do about John? Things were getting worse at home and he still didn't have a job. He needed some metaphorical bends in the road to keep him focused, but how were we going to supply them? How was I to turn these results into a practical solution for John? The answer came from Christine . . .

Christine, a gentle seventy-year-old lady from the fenlands north of Cambridge, had had a stroke affecting the right side of her brain that had left her not only partly paralysed on the left side of her body but also with what is called 'spatial neglect'. In this strange condition, people behave as if the left side of the world does not exist. They may, for instance, read only the right side of the newspaper page, eat food only from the right side of the plate and only speak to people sitting to their right.

Then one day, partly on a hunch, partly guided by my earlier research, I discovered that I could get Christine to pay attention to the left by making a random noise by a handclap or buzzer.

We found that this worked, too, with others suffering spatial neglect, and published the resulting study in the science journal *Nature*.[15] The main idea behind this study was that the unexpected sounds boosted the alertness of the patients and that, because this alertness was controlled by the right half of the brain, it simultaneously improved the patients' ability to pay attention to the left side of space. Perhaps something similar could work with John.

In the meantime, Tom Manly and I discovered another test that uncovered John's difficulties. We designed a virtual job for him on the computer. It was as a pretend hotel receptionist who had been given five different tasks, none of which could be finished in half an hour, far less in the fifteen minutes we allocated for all of them. One job was proofreading leaflets; the second was sorting out the charity coins into different currency denominations; the third was organizing delegate tags for a conference; a fourth was compiling individual hotel bills; and the fifth was looking up telephone numbers for a marketing exercise. We told John that he could never finish one task in the time, but that he had to do equal amounts of work on each of the five main tasks. A perfect performance would mean spending three minutes on the coins, three on the conference labels, and so on.

Actually, most jobs are like this. You have to do a number of things – keeping metaphorical balls in the air – without ever having time to fully finish one task. In fact, this is true of life in general – we skip from activity to activity, juggling different demands and coming back to tasks when we can. John was very bad at this, which is why he felt so stressed.

Sure enough, when we gave him the test – called the Hotel Test – John did badly at it. Even though he was facing a large clock, he seemed to forget completely to check how long he was spending on each task and so didn't move on to the next one. His scatterbrain tendencies which had so frustrated his wife Jane were in full sight here at last: for example, he became immersed in sorting out the charity coins, spending a full eight minutes doing this, before suddenly seeming to remember that there was more to be done and moving on to the conference labels, which he proceeded to spend another five minutes doing. In the remaining two minutes, he rushed to look up some telephone numbers. He did no proofreading and made up no bills. No wonder he couldn't hold down a job.

Now it was time to supply some bends in the road for John's brain. Our 'bends' were the random sounds of a buzzer ringing briefly six times over the fifteen minutes. To our delight, simply making this meaningless interrupting noise was enough to turn John from a scatterbrain to a near-perfect worker in the fake hotel reception. He attempted all five main tasks, spending roughly equal amounts of time on each. Ringing a buzzer was the bend in the road that helped John perform normally. We went on to test this method with ten other people with problems similar to John's: it worked for them, too.[16]

So we had managed to help John become better organized – but only for fifteen minutes. What use was our test going to be when he was at home trying to look after his young children? This is where Christine came in. We had made her more alert and able to attend to what was happening to her left by ringing a buzzer, but we had also managed to find a way of helping her learn to do this for herself. It was a simple method and worked like this.

First we discussed with Christine how she tended to lose focus and 'drift off'. Her daughters found it quite disconcerting that in the middle of visiting hour, for instance, she would sometimes slip into a sort of daze. Gradually Christine also became aware that this could happen, and when she realized what she was doing, it distressed her.

'Your daughters said that you tend to "drift off" when they're with you, Christine?'

'So they tell me – I don't know I'm doing it at the time, but sometimes I find them all looking at me and realize my mind has been somewhere else.'

'Why do you think this happens?'

'I don't really know . . . I suppose I'm a bit dozy since I had the stroke.'

'Can I try something, Christine? – I'm going to clap my hands.'

She looked at me quizzically.

'Whatever floats your boat,' she chuckled. I gave a loud clap. She gave a slight start and looked over at me.

'Did that make you feel any different?' I asked.

'Made me sort of wake up,' she said.

'More alert?' I ventured.

'Yeah, that's it – like I've had a cup of strong coffee.'

'Can I try it a few more times?'

'Fire ahead.'

I waited until she slipped back into her typical round-shouldered dreaminess, then clapped again. Her head lifted and the dreamy cloud cleared. After another few trials, I said: 'Do you think you could learn to do that yourself?'

'Clap my hands?'

'Well, no, I mean – give yourself that feeling without me doing anything?'

'I suppose so – how?'

'You can clap your hands if you want, but it's maybe easier to do these three things. First, sit up really straight, then take a deep breath, and finally I would like you to say a word or phrase to yourself that captures the way you feel when you are alert. Can you think of something to say?'

'Wake up,' she said without hesitation.

'Great, could you do this word search game, and any time you feel you are drifting off, could you do these three things? If I notice you losing concentration, and you don't remember to, I'll remind you.'

Christine's attention drifted after a couple of minutes, but she didn't seem to notice. I reminded her by tapping her shoulder, and after a brief pause, she sat upright, took a deep breath and said 'wake up!' loudly.

'Did that work?' I asked.

'It did,' she smiled, 'I'm wide awake.'

Over the course of the next half-hour or so, Christine would go through her self-alerting routine with only occasional reminders from me. Over a few visits, she learned to do this to the point where it became like a habit she hardly had to think about. Her concentration got much better and she also missed much less on the left side, meaning that she was less likely to have dangerous falls through not noticing things in her path. Christine's daughters were impressed by the fact that their mother seemed much more 'on the ball', but were relieved when she stopped suddenly saying 'wake up!' in the middle of a conversation and instead learned to say it to herself.

This very simple technique worked because a straight posture increases arousal in the brain, as does a deep breath. Saying the word helps create what's known as an 'attentional set' in the brain, in other words a plan or intention, in this case to focus attention. I developed this method into a therapy which we found worked with other people with spatial neglect, one that rehabilitation therapists can teach their patients in the course of their routine therapy.[17]

So we tried this method with John. His catchphrase was 'Focus!' and he learned, every few minutes in the day, to stop what he was doing, say *'Focus!'* to himself, sit up straight and think about what he was supposed to be doing. At first he often found himself in a panic when he realized that he had not checked what his very active three-year-old son was up to in the next room, but gradually, using this deceptively simple mental strategy, he became much less scatterbrained. He never managed to return to his work as a cameraman, but he did get a part-time job in a local bar. He always had to use his mental bend-in-the-road strategy, again and again, whatever he was doing. But it became a habit for him that didn't interfere with his everyday activities. Life at home became a lot less stressful, his children were a lot safer and his marriage survived.

Daniel Kahneman had shown that any mental bends in the road – any challenge, in other words – widened the pupils of the eyes and made the brain rise to the challenge. Gary Aston-Jones and his colleagues at Princeton found in animals that the tiny little LC sprayed the brain with noradrenaline when they noticed something important – an event, a thought, an emotion. But was there a link between these two things – the LC and its noradrenaline on the one hand, and Kahneman's dilated pupils on the other?

It wasn't until 2013 that my colleagues at Trinity College Dublin, Peter Murphy, Josh Balsters, Redmond O'Connell and I found that missing link. We gave a group of volunteers a simple attention task, as they lay in our MRI scanner, and measured their pupil diameters as they did it. Over forty-five minutes or so, the volunteers had to watch a series of blobs on the screen above their heads and press a button when the occasional bigger blob appeared. It was a boring task, with relatively low mental challenge, so not surprisingly the width of their pupils waxed and waned over the course of the experiment. But here was *our* challenge: could we detect that missing link between activity in the brain's only source of noradrenaline – that tiny, two-millimetre-wide thread of cells in the stem of the brain – and the volunteers' pupils' activity?

We could. The LC's firing rose and fell in line with the pupils' widening and narrowing. What's more, when one of the targets appeared, both pupils and LC rose to this minor challenge – this small bend in the road. It was the first time that this sort of connection had been shown in the human brain between noradrenaline and pupil dilation.[18]

Now, we couldn't be sure that this is what had happened in John's brain because I had seen him years before we discovered the noradrenaline–pupil link. But we did try to get a little closer to his brain activity by using the sweatiness of the skin as a proxy for noradrenaline activity. This is an innocuous mini-version of the so-called *fight or flight response*, a collection of responses in the body's sympathetic nervous system that prepares the person to deal with danger or challenge.

Noradrenaline is a key hormone in this chain of events, one of which is the release of sweat from the sweat glands, in readiness to cool a body in case it has to fight or run away fast. Tiny changes in skin sweatiness go reasonably hand in hand with the rise and fall of noradrenaline in the brain, and so can be used as a crude marker of its activity. This is what we had discovered happens to the pupil of the eye – if you find something or someone interesting, difficult, attractive or frightening, your pupils will widen because of a shot of noradrenaline.[19, 20, 21]

Which is how we came to meet Sally, who had been diagnosed with ADHD as an adult. She told me that she wished she had received the diagnosis as a child, because she had found school such a torture of boredom and was distressed by her own distractibility and impulsiveness. I met Sally because she volunteered to take part in a test of a type of alertness training which had arisen out of the work we had done with the head-injured cameraman John.

My colleague Redmond O'Connell and I had decided to help people like Sally with ADHD by using the sweaty skin test as a signal of their alertness. When something new, surprising, interesting or emotional happens, not only do your pupils dilate but your skin becomes slightly sweatier. Even doing mental arithmetic will have this effect, as Daniel Kahneman showed. Suppose we were to show people with ADHD how sweaty their skin was moment to moment on a moving graph on a computer screen. This is a type of what's called 'biofeedback'.

Biofeedback means giving a person information about some activity in their body or brain which they would not normally be aware of – for instance, heart rate, blood pressure or tension in a particular group of muscles. It turns out that simply by becoming aware of these signals, you can often learn to *control* them, by a trial and error process that researchers still don't fully understand. But the moment-to-moment feedback about the signal – heart rate, for instance – allows you to try out various ways of lowering or raising your heartbeat and eventually many people find a way to do that, often in their own odd ways which they can't quite explain, even to themselves. People only had to see their skin conductance move slowly up and down on the computer screen to get the hang of it quite quickly. Here's how we taught Jean, one of our ADHD volunteers.

'Jean, do you see that moving line?'

She nodded.

'That's the sweatiness of the skin on your fingers where these two electrodes are taped. If you're bored or drowsy, the line will go down, and if you're excited or frightened, it will shoot up. And if you are just plain alert, it will be somewhere in the middle. Get it?'

'Yep,' she said, her eyes fixed on the line as it unwound across the screen.

'Now, sometime in the next couple of minutes, I am going to clap my hands behind your back here. You OK with that?'

'Fine,' she said.

I watched the line slowly drop as the minutes passed – Jean was beginning to squirm a little in her chair because she was restless and bored. Then I clapped my hands with a crack behind her head.

'Whoa!' she said, looking round at me.

'Look at the screen,' I said.

The line was making a Mount Everest-like peak on the screen. We sat quietly watching it subside back to base camp. As I had done with Christine, I repeated it a few more times with Jean. Each time, the graph spiked.

'Now you try to do it?'

'What do you mean?' she asked.

'I want you to control your brain by making a spike in your skin sweatiness.'

'How?'

'Remember what it felt like after I clapped my hands? – Try to imagine that feeling in your own head, and try to recreate it.'

I watched as Jean struggled to gain control of her brain's arousal system. For a while nothing happened, and she began some restless shuffling in her seat.

'There!' she shouted, pointing to a hump emerging out of the flat rolling line.

'Great!' I said, 'now try again, and try to make them bigger.'

It took Jean less than twenty minutes before she was creating Matterhorn-like spikes in her skin conductance trace, again and again.

'This is amazing,' she said, 'am I really controlling my brain?'

'You certainly are, Jean – we think you are giving it little spurts of a sort of natural alerting drug that your own body produces, called noradrenaline.'

'Cool, so I can make my own drugs?'

'Yep, and what you have to do is to learn to give yourself a shot just before you have to do something important where you don't want to screw up.'

'Like when I have to proofread my monthly report for my boss.'

'You've got it. You probably have to give yourself a few shots while you are doing that.'

'And when I have to go to my boyfriend's mother's house for dinner – I'm for ever blurting out stupid things that upset her, and then me and the boyfriend have an argument.'

'Sounds like you really will have to dose yourself up then,' I laughed.

After about half an hour of this feedback, we found that almost all of our ADHD volunteers like Jean and Sally could give themselves little 'jolts' of arousal. Because we didn't know at the time that pupil dilation could be used as a measure of noradrenaline activity, we couldn't prove it, but we guessed that Jean, Sally and our other volunteers were learning to give themselves 'shots' of noradrenaline. We also discovered that, when people did this repeatedly, their concentration levels improved and they made many fewer impulsive mistakes, such as pressing the space bar for the number 3 in the SART.[22]

Now, each 'shot' only lasted a few seconds and we were under no illusion that we were permanently increasing noradrenaline levels in Sally's brain. What we were trying to do was to train ADHD volunteers like her to perform a sort of natural 'self-medication', that is, give themselves little boosts of noradrenaline (we suspected) at key times where they had figured out, with our help, that absent-mindedness or impulsiveness might get them into trouble.

Sally gradually learned to recognize these danger times for zoning out. For her, these were times when there were no particular challenges and only the humdrum routine of work. But routine or not, she had a responsible job and needed to focus on the report she had to write or the meeting that had to be minuted. Mostly this intelligent woman could easily do these tasks, but it was their very easiness that posed the greatest risk that her attention would drift and she would goof and cost her company dear.

So Sally learned to recognize these danger times – when she had to do routine but important tasks at work – and would trigger her self-alert strategy before, and then repeatedly during, the task, giving her brain these ultra-natural and ultra-safe 'fixes' of noradrenaline to help maintain its focus and avoid mistakes. Sally also learned to do this in meetings where she had a tendency to drift off and lose track of discussions. This helped her to perform better at work and even to enjoy it more because, as you will see later, boredom tends to lower your mood.

Along with my PhD student Simona Salomone, Redmond and I showed that this was not only true for Sally, but for a large group of people with similar problems. Three months after they had finished the self-alert training, most showed a very significant drop in inattention and impulsiveness compared to a group who had a placebo training programme. What's more, they showed fewer signs of depression and performed better on attention tests.[23]

I had discovered that challenge played a key role in cameraman John's troubles and had managed to capture these problems in the laboratory by the mistakes he made on the SART. Years of research meant I now understood quite well the way this worked in the brain. The broader question now arose: in what situations does this challenge have positive effects and help us all cope with adversity, and in what situations does it sabotage us? The stories of John, Sally and Christine and the research they were a part of, laid the groundwork for me to go on to find the answer to this question.

Out of darkness can come light. Had Ruth Holland not died in that rail crash back in 1996, I might never have embarked on the long journey that ended up with my finding a way to help Sally, Christine, John and people like them to find their own brain-enhancing challenges – their own individual bends in the road, so to speak.

As a clinical psychologist, I felt good that my long research journey had produced something useful. But as a scientist, I still wasn't satisfied that I understood when, why and how challenge makes us, and when it breaks us. It took an earthquake in New Zealand to help me answer that question.

2

What a New Zealand Earthquake
Taught Me About Nietzsche

It was 4.35 a.m. on 4 September 2010 when the earth began to shudder and the citizens of Christchurch, New Zealand, tumbled from their sleep out into the streets. The 7.1 magnitude earthquake heaved, groaned and bucked ten kilometres below them. Buildings lurched and cracked and power and water supplies failed, yet no one was killed. But they were tormented for weeks afterwards by hundreds of aftershocks that again and again sent people, pulses racing and pupils dilated with fear, out into the streets.

After the earthquake, many found it hard to concentrate on their work and ordinary activities. They forgot appointments, couldn't remember the name of the person they had just met, were paralysed with indecisions as small as what kind of coffee to buy and felt mentally slowed and fuzzy. Just about anyone under a lot of stress can have these sorts of problems, but it was the earthquake that filled and muddled the Christchurch citizens' minds.

Deak Helton and his colleagues from the University of Christchurch[1] had spotted these reactions to the disaster and quickly set about assessing psychologically a group of

Christchurch students. While some had no problems, others couldn't stop thinking about the danger and risk they had faced, with images of the earthquake flashing through their minds.

Curiously, Helton also asked them to complete the SART that I had developed at Cambridge – the one which had finally pinned down cameraman John's problems. Helton discovered something quite strange: the students who made the most mistakes on the SART were the ones who were most distracted and tormented by the earthquake.

I was intrigued by his results. Why should the SART predict how upset you are after an earthquake? A first common-sense answer is that worry is distracting and so makes you lose concentration. But there is a problem with that explanation, I realized, after I remembered something quite embarrassing that happened to me years earlier.

I was a postgraduate student in London and someone asked me if I could help with a television programme about the effects of alcohol on driving. The idea was that we would do an experiment in front of a studio audience showing how alcohol disrupts brain function by giving volunteers cognitive tests before and after a dose of alcohol. They were randomly assigned to two groups and, while they all thought they had been given alcohol, in fact half had actually been given a placebo disguised to taste like alcohol. The real-alcohol group would make lots more mistakes and have slower reaction times than the placebo group, or so we confidently predicted.

As planned, we carried out the experiments with the volunteers and the programme was recorded for later broadcast. Before they drank their alcohol or placebo, each group did equally well on our tests. And, sure enough, after their drinks, one group did better than the other on the second set of tests.

The director gave us a grateful thumbs-up. This programme had been done on a shoestring without much time for preparation and he had clearly worried that we might not find any differences.

Except . . . the wrong group did better.

To our dismay, we realized that the fake alcohol group's performance had got worse, while the alcohol group's hadn't changed. We braved the producer's tense glare as we anxiously re-analysed the results, but, no, they were completely opposite to those we had predicted. Not that this made any difference to the television people. I assumed that the director and his team would have to explain the contrary finding or not broadcast. Not at all – I found out later that they did broadcast, reporting the actual numbers from the tests as if they confirmed the prediction about the bad effects of alcohol on performance, and no one noticed!

We escaped to the pub for a debriefing. Why did the alcohol group show no difference in their reaction times, when we know that alcohol actually does worsen performance and increase accidents? As we sipped our beer, licking the wounds of our battered scientific egos, it suddenly came to me. How could I have forgotten one of the most famous experiments in psychology?

The Two-Edged Sword of Stress

In 1908, Harvard psychologists Robert Yerkes and John Dodson discovered what became known as the Yerkes–Dodson law of arousal.[2] 'Arousal' is the term used to describe the level of general background activity in a physiological system. We tend to use it with respect to sex, where high arousal means increased activity in the glands, hormones and organs linked to sex. But arousal has a more general meaning in psychology, and roughly corresponds to the idea of 'alertness' which I explained in the last chapter, and this in turn is closely linked to the chemical messenger noradrenaline and its widened pupils, slightly dampened skin and beating heart.

Our arousal levels fluctuate throughout the day and night and tend to be low in the pre-dawn hours and high in the late morning. Yerkes and Dodson found that if you increase arousal up to a certain point, performance gets better. But then there is a tipping point at which further increases in arousal cause a slump in performance. This is the classic Yerkes–Dodson 'inverted U' curve of arousal.

That, we realized, was probably what had happened to our volunteers in the television studio. Being tested under bright lights and cameras in front of an audience in the unfamiliar atmosphere of a television studio is stressful. That stress increased arousal in all the volunteers and that in turn pushed the placebo volunteers over the far side of the Yerkes–Dodson curve and made them worse.

Alcohol calms us down and so brought down the arousal levels of the alcohol group of volunteers, hauling them back up to the top of the Yerkes–Dodson performance curve. That explained our embarrassing TV studio results – too much stress had pushed the placebo group beyond their Yerkes–Dodson peak of performance, while alcohol had neutralized some of the stress for that group and so rescued them from that downside of the curve.

This was the first hint that something interesting was going on in New Zealand. If the Yerkes–Dodson inverted U-curve of performance versus stress was to hold in New Zealand as it seemed to on the TV study, then some people who were at the peak of this 'stress curve' as a result of the earthquake should have actually performed better on SART. This wasn't the case, however. Was there any research to back up this idea? Indeed there was, I discovered.

In 2008 Sian Beilock of Chicago University gave students arithmetic problems and chose a group who were all equally good at them. She then assessed how nervous they felt about their arithmetical abilities and found that some of them were anxious about arithmetic, despite the fact that they were objectively good at it.

Imagine someone asks you to do mental arithmetic problems in front of an audience – most of us would find this pretty stressful. Beilock asked her students to do exactly this and she not only looked at how well they performed on the problems, but also measured levels of the stress hormone cortisol before and after the session.[3]

It wasn't a surprise that cortisol levels shot up in both the maths-anxious and the maths-non-anxious students – public performance is stressful. But that's where the similarities ended.

In the maths-anxious group, the more stressed students were, the worse they performed on the problems. This is no surprise for anyone who has seen very clever students underperform badly under exam stress. Stress disrupts our mental abilities, doesn't it?

Actually, no it doesn't – not always, anyway.

Here is the extraordinary thing which happened with the maths-non-anxious group who were, as you will recall, no better at arithmetic than their maths-anxious fellow students: *the more of the stress hormone cortisol they produced, the BETTER they performed.*

What doesn't kill me really *can* make me not only stronger, but also *better*. But not for everyone: if you worry about and doubt your ability, this has the opposite effect – it *weakens* your performance. But if you don't worry about your ability, *stress can boost your performance* – and in this case the more of it the better. Stress pushed them up into an optimal zone of performance, in other words.

Here was Yerkes–Dodson in action, a hundred years later, uncovering the two-edged sword of stress in action in twenty-first-century classrooms. Cortisol – the classic stress hormone – had opposite effects in the maths-anxious students than in the non-anxious ones: more stress meant *worse* performance in the first, but *better* in the second – even though their actual mathematical abilities were the same. Stress, in other words, seemed to push non-worriers into a performance sweet spot and worriers out of it.

Stress, I had discovered, is a two-edged sword – it can distract and inhibit you, or it can boost your abilities and push you nearer to optimal performance – just like a bend in a long, straight road. But most performers and sports people know this already: if they don't feel that edge of anxiety before the game, then they won't perform at their best. The golfer Tiger Woods captures this when he says: 'The day I'm not nervous is the day I quit . . . That's the greatest thing about it, just to feel that rush.'

So maybe the New Zealand students who were stressed by the earthquake didn't make more mistakes on the SART *just* because of their distracting worries. It was a factor for some, but Yerkes and Dodson told us that some of them should actually do better with the stress. The results didn't show that, however. So what else might explain this relationship between emotional distress and attention?

A few thousand SMS messages helped me answer this question.

A Wandering Mind Is an Unhappy Mind

The SMS signal in your phone bleeps. A question on the screen: *How are you feeling right now?* You choose a number from between 0 (very bad) to 100 (very good).

Another question: *What are you doing right now?* You scroll through and click from the choices.

Then the final question appears: *Are you thinking about something other than what you're currently doing?* You thumb one of four options – No. Yes – something pleasant. Yes – something neutral. Yes – something unpleasant.

More than two thousand people signed up to allow Matthew Killingsworth and Dan Gilbert of Harvard University to send them these messages at random times, roughly three times per day for a few weeks.[4]

People's minds wander a lot: as the replies came pinging back, they gave the intriguing picture of 2,000 minds wandering roughly *half* the time. And here is the even stranger fact: it didn't matter whether they were doing a really grungy home chore like cleaning the bathroom, or sipping cocktails on the sun-drenched deck of a yacht – minds were equally likely to wander to good, bad or neutral things whatever the activity.

Not only that, but a wandering mind was almost always less happy than a mind focused on what it was doing – *even if drudgery was being done!* You might think – ah, but if I am sitting on the yacht, sipping a Manhattan while dolphins frolic under the gleaming white hull, how could my daydreams not make me happy?

Wrong. People are no happier during pleasant daydreams than when their minds are focused on scrubbing the lavatory.

What's the reason for this? Does mind wandering make you less happy? Or, when your mood dips, does that make your mind wander? Which comes first, the mind-wandering chicken or the mood egg?

The answer? The chicken wins. The researchers tracked people's mood hour by hour, day by day, over several weeks, and so could see which came first – changes in mind wandering or changes in mood. Mind wandering came first. If you let your mind wander a lot, you'll make yourself unhappier, sun-drenched yacht or no sun-drenched yacht.

So, were the Christchurch students who were bad at SART more stressed because their minds tended to wander more to earthquake worries? This made sense, because by the late noughties, by which time I had moved to Dublin, laboratories around the world were using SART to measure mind wandering.

One piece of research from North Carolina caught my attention.[5] They gave the SART to seventy-two adults and then asked them to record their moods, thoughts and mind wanderings eight times per day for the following week, using similar methods to the Harvard researchers. Just as I had predicted for the Christchurch students, those who were poor at SART in the lab were much more likely to mind-wander as they went about their lives during the next week. What's more, these daydream-prone people found that their minds wandered to worries more than pleasant thoughts and that this often got in the way of what they were trying to do.

So in New Zealand it wasn't that post-earthquake stress caused some to do badly on SART, rather that mind-wandering-prone people were worse at SART with or without stress. Their difficulty in keeping focused caused *both* their bad SART scores *and* their vulnerability to stress after the earthquake.

A wandering mind, then, is indeed an unhappy mind. If you can focus on your day-to-day tasks and save your daydreaming for when you choose, you will be able to cope with the sorts of stresses that earthquake victims suffer much better than if you are a mind wanderer.

Resilience, then, needs *focus*. If you can keep your mind on the moment-to-moment tasks of ordinary life, you'll shield yourself from extra stress which saps your energy and hence your strength.

There was something which was bothering me, though – why do our minds tend to wander towards bad things?

Why Do Our Minds Wander To Unhappy Thoughts?

Why shouldn't my attention drift to nice, happy thoughts? That question made me remember Simon, one of my former patients whom I had seen in London in the late seventies.

Simon was in his late forties, a senior official in a national professional association. He was at the peak of his career, often on television, consulted by government and respected by his professional colleagues. He was happily married with three children, with no significant problems in his life. Except for one.

The family doctor referred Simon to me because he had been suffering recurrent bouts of intense anxiety and low mood for the last six months. When I first met him, the dark shadows under his eyes confirmed his doctor's report of many sleepless nights. It was 1978, so he hadn't been prescribed antidepressants. Today he would have had them in a blink.

Simon's life had been fine until, six months previously, one big issue turned up – a phobia about public speaking. He had confused his lines while giving a platform address at a large national conference and had ended the speech early, red-faced and, as he saw it, humiliated in front of his peers. He was due to speak at the same annual conference in six months and the thought of that was crippling him emotionally.

Certain types of severe anxiety can make you very self-centred, especially the fear of people thinking badly of you, or laughing at you. The fear traps you into an egocentric view of the world where it seems as if everyone is looking at you, alive to every tiny flush of your skin, tremor in your voice or awkwardness in your gestures.

Your own internal state is amplified to a point where it seems that others must be able to hear the boom, boom of your pounding heart filling your ears. In this hyper-vigilant state, you scan other people for signs of disapproval, scorn or disappointment. And if you look in any face for long enough you will find such expressions, even though in reality they may be nothing more than a passing stomach cramp in the person concerned.

Your attention system becomes emotionally locked on to these negative thoughts and perceptions which, of course, feed your anxiety even more until eventually it will break through and actually *make* you awkward in your gestures, peculiar in your speech and flushed in your face.

It all boils down to what you focus your attention on.

I had just begun to learn cognitive behaviour therapy. In CBT, you assume that people's thoughts and beliefs cause their emotions. If you believe, as Simon did, that other people are laughing at you and thinking you are incompetent, this is incredibly stressful and will cause you huge anxiety. A key step in CBT is to ask people to seek evidence for their beliefs and this is what I did with Simon.

'What do you think happened at the conference?'

'I dried up . . . it was terrible, so embarrassing, in front of the National Executive and all my junior colleagues – it was the most humiliating meltdown . . .'

'So what happened, exactly?'

'I told you, I just dried up – began to stutter, then suddenly my heart was racing, I was soaked in sweat and I had to hold on to the lectern to stop myself falling because my legs were like jelly.'

'You had just begun to speak?'

'No, no, I was well past halfway . . . I don't know what came over me.'

'So you had given the bulk of your speech?'

'Well . . . yes, I suppose so – but I just . . . just fizzled out – it was absolutely awful!'

'What would the audience have seen?'

'What do you mean?'

'Imagine you were in the audience, looking up at you, what would you have noticed?'

'A stuttering fool unable to speak about to fall over with panic,' he muttered, miserably.

'But what *specifically* would they have noticed?'

'I don't know . . . they would have seen me suddenly stop speaking.'

'Completely?'

'No, not completely, I did sort of limp on and then fizzle out.'

'What else would they have noticed?'

'That I was in a state . . .'

'What sort of state?'

'I was near to fainting, I thought I was going to have a heart attack!'

'But what could they see?'

'I don't know . . . they could see I wasn't . . . normal.'

'They couldn't see your heart beat . . . or see your sweaty hands . . . or know that you were feeling dizzy?'

'No, I suppose not . . . but they knew I had come to a sudden end.'

'OK, so I'd like you to do something before next week – I want you to think of a few people at the conference who you know well enough to ask to tell you honestly what they noticed – people you haven't talked to about it.'

'I haven't talked to anyone.'

'Fine, who will you ask?'

After some thought and with some reluctance, he named some colleagues and the session ended. He came back the next week with the news that, of the four people he had asked, only two said they had noticed anything out of the ordinary in his speech; one of them thought he had had a dizzy spell and the other that he had had to stop because he was not feeling well. None of the four realized that he had had an anxiety attack.

I had edged Simon out of his egocentric, blinkered nest of fear and forced him to change to a different perspective on the conference speech. I had helped him change his focus of attention from one locked on to his internal world of anxiety and out into a much more realistic – and indeed largely indifferent – world.

'Simon, you have to remember that most people spend most of the time thinking about themselves. They don't have the mental space to be scrutinizing every other person's face for what's going on inside their heads,' I told him one day.

But Simon was a perfectionist who had known only success in his life. His anxiety had lifted a bit, but he still had quite a few problems. For him, the fluffed speech was a humiliating stain on his public and self-image. Now his work – and indeed his family life – were suffering because his anxiety was sabotaging his performance. These further failures caused him yet more angst.

This is the vicious cycle that can kindle anxiety into a blaze of emotion which can feel like it is consuming you. This is what happened to Lucy – the relatively small setback of a failed exam caused anxiety that then incubated in exactly the same way as Simon's conference setback.

And at the root of this vicious cycle is . . . *attention*.

When we are anxious, our mind becomes like a missile defence system on the watch for incoming threats. And because there is so much going on around us, and with the sensitivity of the system turned up high enough, it will always find a potential threat, however tiny.

It also skews our memory. In an anxious mood, worry-linked memories spring more easily to mind than happy, confident memories. So it becomes harder and harder to turn our attention to positive thoughts, signs and memories because our anxious, egocentric world is populated only by anxiety-raising signs (that person is laughing . . . at me?), thoughts (I might faint . . .) and memories (the feeling of that awful moment when I dried up).

Eventually I worked out that Simon had become not only a public-speaking phobic, but also a failure phobic. His attention flashed to the slightest reminder of the forthcoming conference, or any suggestion that he might be required to give a speech. Furthermore, normal, everyday mini-failures were threats that his anti-missile attention system locked on to. And then

I remembered one key fact about attention – things you pay attention to look bigger.

Attention is, almost literally, a magnifying glass for the mind. Depression makes you recall unhappy events and attention then magnifies them. Simon's focus on many little trivial mini-failures gradually magnified them into one big rolling failure that had been kicked off by that public speaking humiliation.

His skewed attention had even spread to his relationship with his family and colleagues. In his anxious state, it homed in on trivial comments or facial expressions that he would never have noticed in his normal state. Nor would he have interpreted them in the way he was doing now – as signs that his colleagues, even his wife, considered him a failure, too. That led him to start cutting himself off, which of course made his anxiety worse and made it harder for his distorted attention to find alternatives to the 'I am a failure' message which it was now drip-feeding into Simon's mind.

But, luckily for Simon, he wasn't absent-minded and had a great ability to focus his attention on what he was doing: he wasn't normally a mind wanderer and so could focus on the goals I set him without being derailed too much by his anxiety.

We began the behaviour part of CBT by gradually getting Simon used to preparing for speeches, and then, eventually, giving brief speeches to me in more and more formal situations. I had him mentally rehearse the steps leading up to the big speech and then give the talk out loud to himself at home several times. In our final test he had to present it in a lecture hall to me and three students who I recruited for the purpose. His phobia abated, just in time for the conference – and he made the speech, albeit with, as he described it, 'a few hairy moments' during it.

But I also had to tackle his failure phobia. I taught him firstly to take note when his attention was wandering towards memories of his supposed 'failures'. Then he learned to refocus his attention on the more accurate evidence that he was, in fact, a considerable success. It did not take Simon long to learn to catch himself in the act of reliving the fluffed conference speech, and, with some difficulty at first, replacing that memory with one of the many successes he had had in his life. He also learned to pay attention to people's positive reactions towards him and not to focus on the tiny, usually ambiguous, responses that he had assumed were signs of disapproval.

Once he had learned to refocus his attention away from signs and memories linked to failure – or, better still, never get attracted to them in the first place – his mood improved and his anxiety dropped. That in turn made positive memories much more likely to spring into his mind and so he didn't need to fight off the down-drag of worry nearly as much.

And because Simon's focus was good, once he had his emotions under better control, failure and anxiety thoughts found it harder to edge into his consciousness. Of course they did from time to time, but by then he had learned to refocus his attention on positive evidence of his success in life and could quite easily prevent them taking hold like before.

If Simon had been absent-minded on the other hand, it would have been harder for him to stop his mind wandering. And, as I have already said, when the mind goes walkabout it is likely to end up in worry and negativity. After the Christchurch earthquake, the minds of the New Zealanders who had poorer focus wandered more than those of their peers – to worries about the earthquake.

I was reminded by an experience in my own life which gave me the intuition that there is at least one other thing with an equivalent pull to that of an earthquake. It was the torture of the piping party.

A piping party consists of a group of sailors each blowing on a bosun's whistle to 'pipe up' or 'pipe down' the flag, greet important guests on board ship and so on. This four-inch-long instrument emits a piercing whistle if the four fingers of the hand are cupped in just the right shape above the open mouth of a little round bowl that sits at the end of the whistle. If the fingers don't quite make the right shape, then the piercing single-note whistle transmutes into an off-key multi-note screech.

Worse, this abysmal invention can generate not one, but two notes – the aforementioned high-pitched whistle and also a second, lower note, achieved by a slightly different cupping of the fingers around its little bowl. If a wrongly blown first note could bring tears of pain to the eye, a mispiped second note – more flatulent rasp than whistle – was more likely to elicit hysterical laughter.

But we were not, as thirteen-year-old boys, sea-hardened sailors – we were the piping party of the 29th Glasgow Sea Scouts. And I was the newly made leader of the piping party – a position of high responsibility and some esteem. At the beginning of every Friday evening meeting, my piping party whistled up the flag and, at the end, we piped it down.

Simple enough, you might think. For sure, there was always someone in the party who blew the toe-curlingly wrong note but it was never much of a problem as its effects were diluted by the other pipers. No, the awful addition to this very public ritual was the 'dismiss' two-note whistle that the leader of the party – me – had to blow after the flag was up or after it was down.

When I had practised this before taking up my new senior role, it had always worked beautifully – two notes, an octave apart, as pure as a thrush's call. But the first time I had to dismiss the party, I emitted a screech which drew tears from sixty pairs of eyes, closely followed by the sound of what can only be described as a tremulously blown fart.

Shocked silence filled the Scout hall before some disloyal compatriot began to giggle, which was the cue for a collapse into general hilarity, even among the adult Scoutmasters. The humiliation I felt was an acutely physical sensation – I can still feel the blood rushing to my cheeks and the awful twisting in my stomach as sixty people laughed at me.

By the next morning I had forgotten about it and got on with my adolescent business. But when I woke up the next Friday morning, there was something gnawing at my stomach that I realized was anxiety about my performance that all too rapidly approaching evening. My heart was pounding and my thoughts full of dread as we marched up to the pole for the flag-raising ceremony. The six pipes piped it up. Then a dreadful silence prevailed – and to my painfully tuned-in mind, I realized with a ghastly insight that every single person in that hall was waiting with malicious glee for my dismiss whistle. I did not disappoint. When the sounds came, a small bird was first cruelly tortured and then noisily crushed. Ah, how they laughed!

It was on Thursday morning the following week that I woke up with a thick plug of anxiety in my throat. For the next thirty-six hours I experienced multiple little panic attacks as I rehearsed in my mind the likely outcome of that Friday's performance. I could hardly concentrate at school as my mind replayed the sounds and images of humiliation.

Of course, there could be nothing else but a self-fulfilling prophecy in this macabre dance between anxiety and perfor-mance: had you stripped out the anxiety, I would have piped as pure as a sandpiper on the sandflats at dawn. And as the weeks went on – I can only assume that some sort of sadism lay behind the decision not to relieve me of my tortured command – the day of my anxiety advanced from Thursday to Wednesday to Tuesday and so on until for a whole week I was being stretched on the rack of anxiety.

Concentration was so hard. If ever I managed to lose myself in French verbs or algebra, the moment my attention lapsed the ridiculous panic about a silly Friday night performance would set in. And I could not get it out of my head: anxiety is a truly horrible experience – it is meant to be acute and short-lived, motivating us to escape from danger, but our imagination-rich brains can turn it into the most prolonged mental torture by constant replays and anticipation of the 'danger'.

I don't know how long this went on for. All I can remember are several months of acute distress. Perhaps the summer break came and I no longer had to do it. Whatever was the case, once I no longer had to pipe on a Friday night, the anxiety evaporated. It was as if someone had given me an amazing new drug which eliminated a distress that had consumed my waking hours and haunted my sleeping ones, too.

What a trivial thing to be so anxious about, you might think. Hardly a 'what doesn't kill me' scenario that would have impressed Nietzsche. Quite the reverse – my response had been out of all proportion to any objective source of stress. The anxiety that I incubated had tipped me over the far side of the Yerkes–Dodson curve so that it was inevitable I would blow awful sounds of a Friday night and experience my weekly humiliation.

I had worked out one reason for this 'incubation': after something stressful happens – whether a public-speaking flop, a piping party debacle or an earthquake – our threat-detecting 'missile defence system' goes on to hyper-alert to search for more threats. And if our minds are unfocused and wandering, they will drift quickly to the threat and so amplify our anxiety and stress. Thus is the sort of vicious cycle set off that I saw in my client Simon, experienced myself as a failed piping party leader and am sure happened to some of the earthquake victims.

But here is a puzzle: my sustained attention is actually quite good. Even as an adolescent, I could usually concentrate well and wasn't a habitual mind wanderer. Yet during those few months of stress in the Sea Scouts, my mind didn't just wander – whenever my attention drifted for just a moment, it would sprint like a greyhound after these bad memories of my humiliation. But if attention protects you against mind wandering to negative thoughts, and I had quite good attention, why was I being tormented by them?

And then it came to me. I realized what it was about these memories that rattled me so much. I saw what was at the core of all these horrible, distracting, panic-inducing thoughts and memories. It was *me*.

For most of the day our attention is on the *outside* – on other people, on events, actions, future plans and so on. But sometimes our focus changes to *inside* – to our own selves. The term 'self-consciousness' has negative connotations of social awkwardness, but you can be aware of yourself in positive ways as well, such as when you notice that you're making a good impression on someone. Simon, for instance, who had the public speaking phobia, was so self-conscious that he assumed others could see the invisible feelings of anxiety inside him. Because *his* attention was inside himself much of the time, it stopped him paying attention outside where he would have noticed the distracted indifference that is the state of mind of most of the people surrounding us.

We are only consciously aware of a fraction of the things we can possibly attend to. A second ago, for instance, you weren't aware of the pressure of the seat you are sitting on against your lower thighs but, now that I mention it, suddenly you notice it. Or that background hum of traffic that you were quite unconscious of a few moments ago is now in your awareness, simply because I mention it.

The self is more or less just another 'thing' that you may or may not be paying attention to at any one moment. Or is it? Actually, I realized, the self is a rather special 'thing' which can draw our attention more than most things. That, I realized, was the case with the adolescent me. My anxiety was almost entirely centred on *me* and my humiliation in the eyes of others.

Walking up to the flag at the head of the piping party was twenty feet of the most tortured self-consciousness. Every sensation in my body of which I would normally be completely unaware – the thud of my feet on the floorboards, the swinging of my arms, the whistle clenched in my sweaty hand, the tension at the back of my neck, my rapid breath and beating heart – these filled my attention. Then, after the squawk-croak of my whistle, all I was aware of was the laughter of my peers and the pulsing glow on my face.

Adolescents are notoriously self-conscious and brain imaging confirms this. When you focus on the outside world, the outside surface of your brain shows the greatest activity, but when you attend to your interior world, to yourself and your memories, plans, thoughts and fears, it is the *inside* surface of the two halves of your brain which tends to show the greatest activity: you really do literally 'go into yourself' when you start thinking about your self.[6]

If you scan the brains of adolescents and tell them that another teenager of their age and gender is watching them, the inside middle surfaces of their frontal lobes activate much more than is the case for children or adults.[7] This internal focus on the self sucks attention from the outside world, which is partly why teenagers can be so gawky and awkward – and so can anxious adults like Simon and Lucy.

So maybe it takes more than good attention to make you resilient. For tough times to make you stronger, you also have to be able sometimes to de-focus attention from your self and that may involve doing some maintenance work on your self, which I'll come back to in Chapter 6.

I had made some progress in understanding emotional resilience: focus, up to a point, will defend you from the emotional scars of bad experiences. But I can think of many people with all the focus in the world who have not grown stronger when bad things – awful neurological illnesses, for instance – had struck them. I still had not fully cracked emotional resilience and that disappointment made my mind wander – back to 1977, and a well-known London art gallery.

3

Rodin and the Goalkeeper

It's almost four decades ago now and I wish I could boast that I was the one who noticed it first, that day I walked into the Tate Gallery in London in 1977 and saw Rodin's *The Kiss* for the first time. But it was my friend Sam, an art buff, who drew my attention to it: the life-sized naked couple strained hungrily towards each other, sexuality radiating from the cold marble.

'Do you notice anything?' he asked.

'Erm . . . they're enjoying themselves?' I ventured.

He raised his eyebrows – I was most certainly not an art buff – and quizzed me: 'What direction are they turning in?'

I studied the pair.

'Right – they're both turning to the right . . . but so what?'

'Follow me,' Sam said smugly, as I trailed after him like a sulky child to another room in the gallery.

We were now standing in front of a pencil drawing, a remarkable evocation of carnal lust – two faces, tongues entwined as if they were trying to eat each other.

'Picasso,' he proclaimed proprietorially. 'He was eighty-six when he drew this. Do you see?'

I peered at the contorted faces in Picasso's drawing, also called *The Kiss*.

'Both turning right,' I said matter-of-factly, 'but, again . . . so what?'

'Follow me,' he sighed.

Now I was standing in front of another drawing – again all tongues and sexual hunger – *The Kiss II* by the Scottish artist John Bellany.

'OK, they're turning right, too. But I'm not sure that three is a statistically significant number,' I muttered, trying to pull scientific rank on my show-off arty friend.

But a couple of hours and a few art books later, he had me convinced. Roy Lichtenstein's *The Kiss*, man and woman again with heads bent to the right. Then an incredible painting by Jean-Léon Gérôme, *Pygmalion and Galatea*, in which the naked, half-marble, half-human model cranes rightward, round and down from her pedestal to kiss her tiptoe right-straining artist . . . and so it went on.

'OK,' I said at last. 'I'm persuaded. So what's your point?'

'You're the psychologist,' Sam said. 'Tell me why so many of them kiss to the right?'

And so he set me on a long and complicated journey to try to find out why all these figures kissed to the right. Strangely enough, much later this also helped me to understand better how people can become stronger with stress.

Sam had intrigued, but not entirely convinced me. The ability of art historians and literary scholars to make sweeping generalizations with complete certainty has always unsettled me. While scientists tend to spend a lot of time trying to test whether their theories are wrong, those in the arts seem devoted to proving their theories and opinions right.

What was missing from Sam's admittedly fascinating tutorial, I realized, was *evidence*. True, he had shown me a dozen paintings and sculptures in which the figures turned to the right, but I didn't know how representative these were of all the kissing artworks in the world. To be sure that his conclusion was correct, I would have to take a random sample of *The Kiss* artworks in the galleries of the world and statistically test the direction of the kisses.

But even if I were to do that and Sam's theory was supported by my findings, what would they tell me? Only that artists prefer to paint and sculpt rightward kisses. I wouldn't be any the wiser about whether ordinary people kiss more to the right than to the left. So I said goodbye to my friend Sam, who was entering the seventh year of his PhD in the History of Art, left London and its galleries and forgot all about his theory of the rightward kiss.

Paul

I moved back home to Scotland and after a few years, in 1984, found myself as a rookie clinical neuropsychologist in a brain rehabilitation centre at the Astley Ainslie Hospital in Edinburgh. During my training I had seen all sorts of people with psychological and psychiatric problems, ranging from schizophrenia through depression to alcoholism. These patients could be emotionally challenging for a young psychologist but, truth be told, I found it much harder to cope emotionally with some of my new patients at the Astley Ainslie.

To see a mother of two young children in her thirties crippled with a progressive Parkinson's disease, or a handsome man in his prime struck down with rapidly advancing multiple sclerosis, or a student of literature, brain-damaged after a fall from a balcony, struggling to string together just a few syllables of the English language – that was very tough indeed.

One reason for this was that I could so easily identify with them. In the most part they had been healthy, normal, well-functioning people before fate had suddenly dealt them a cruel blow. But the more important reason, perhaps, was their acute awareness of their plight and the distress they felt. They could see so clearly the difference between then and now, between their old lives and this new, tough reality; and, unlike many people with psychological and psychiatric conditions, there wasn't a lot that they – or I – could do about it.

But there was one exception to this rule among the patients I met in my new job. One group of people who seemed strangely calm about their disability and among whom an almost – but not quite – Buddhist serenity seemed to prevail as they struggled to learn to navigate their wheelchairs, put on their clothing and muster their limp, paralysed left arms and legs.

I remember in particular Paul, the first person I saw with this problem, whom I first visited in a large, austere ward in a Victorian general hospital. (As with all the patients in the book, Paul's details and name have been changed.) I found this big, strong man in his early seventies in a wheelchair parked side-on to a blank wall near his bed. As I walked towards him, I was struck by his stillness, by the lack of even the slightest head turn or eye flicker in response to the near-constant activity up and down the aisle of the ward.

And still no response as I came up close to him.

'Paul?' I said, repeating his name a second time more loudly when he didn't reply. Slowly he turned his head a fraction towards me – it was as if his neck was stiff. I decided to change sides, with his permission moving his wheelchair away from the wall and sitting on his right side.

Suddenly Paul was talking and responding, telling me about his grandchildren and the carpentry he had taken up since he retired as a civil servant seven years earlier. But the lunch delivery interrupted us and I left, promising to return when he had finished.

When I came back, his plate was half cleared, the right half empty while the left side was covered with uneaten food.

'You weren't hungry, Paul?'

'Oh, I was,' he replied. 'The food isn't bad here – I ate the lot.'

'But your plate . . .' I said, uncertainly.

'Clean as a whistle,' he smiled, looking down at it.

That was the moment at which I decided what I would spend the next part of my professional life working on. Paul was the first person I saw who was suffering from 'unilateral spatial neglect', the same problem that Christine, who I mentioned in Chapter 1, suffered from, and who I was to meet many years later in Cambridge. Spatial neglect is a surprisingly common problem that can arise when certain parts of the brain – most often in the right half – are damaged, usually by a stroke, as was the case with Paul.

I saw a lot of Paul over the next few months, because he was moved to my hospital. He was very slow to recover the use of his left arm and leg – this, I found out, was pretty typical of people with spatial neglect. And I noticed that, when I was talking with him, he would often appear to 'drift off' as if his attention had wandered as Christine's had. But as soon as I said his name, he would come back as normal, friendly and talkative.

Several years would pass before my two colleagues died in the train accidents and my bend-in-the-road research, which I described in Chapter 1, began properly, but it was really Paul who kindled my interest in how attention drifts and the mind wanders.

Warm though my relationship with Paul was, there was always something about him that I couldn't quite put my finger on. It wasn't just the fact that he could drift off mid-conversation – there was also a certain quality to his demeanour, something missing that I couldn't identify. That something nagged at me.

Ken Heilman beamed at me as I stepped out of the taxi into the Florida sunshine at the University of Gainesville campus. One of the world's leading neuropsychologists, this modest man has been one of the key figures in pushing forward an understanding of the brain through his careful studies of brain-damaged patients.

I was due to give a lecture in his department and was chatting with him beforehand when he mentioned a paper he had published a few years earlier that I had not come across. The moment he told me about it, a bell rang – and suddenly I understood what had been niggling at me about Paul.

If you open a magazine and see a shocking picture of a mutilated body, or a sexually explicit image, the pupils of your eyes will widen and the sweat glands in your skin will open up a little – symptoms of boosted arousal, in the general, alertness, Yerkes–Dodson sense – caused by the sympathetic autonomic nervous system. Something similar happens if you touch a hot stove or prick your finger on a needle – pain switches on this same system and makes you super-alert.

Ken, with his long experience of people with spatial neglect, had a hunch about what made them so detached. He tested this by showing patients emotionally arousing, eye-catching pictures like brutal injuries or sexually suggestive interactions.[1] When he did this with healthy people, their skin dampened in response to such emotionally charged images, but not when they saw emotionally neutral pictures.

But people with neglect like Paul were completely different – their skin sweatiness flat-lined, indicating no difference between the neutral and the more emotive pictures. *This* was what I hadn't been able to pinpoint with Paul – a sort of blandness, a lack of emotional *tone* to his interactions with me.

Sure, he was friendly and talkative, but there was no real emotional 'bite' to his conversations. And that gave the impression of a detached, slightly indifferent take-it-or-leave-it approach to life which I only discovered later, after Paul's death, his wife had seen all too clearly and found very painful to endure.

But it was precisely this emotional blankness – this absence of arousal – which made Paul and patients like him seem so much less distressed than my other patients, perhaps revealing my own emotional vulnerability by making me unconsciously attracted to working with them. And Ken Heilman confirmed this by showing that even mild electric shocks to their skin, which caused spikes of arousal in healthy people, also flat-lined in people with spatial neglect:[2] physical pain left them emotionally relatively unperturbed, and so presumably the same was true for both the physical and psychological pain of crippling disability.

So I flew back to Edinburgh and attached Paul – who was by now living at home again – to a portable skin conductance device. Sure enough, when I showed him emotionally loaded pictures, compared to a group of healthy people of his age he hardly showed any response to them, the trace of his skin sweatiness on the computer screen hardly rising.

He recognized the pictures and made comments about them – 'Oh dear, that looks painful' to a grim picture of a deeply cut hand, for instance – but there was little emotional tone in his response. That was because his brain was not triggering an arousal response and that in turn was what was underpinning the strangely indifferent flatness that had puzzled me about Paul before I went to Florida.

But something else was niggling me about him. It came home to me when I found him reading the *Scotsman* newspaper when I visited one morning. 'How's the eyesight?' I asked him, because in the past he had complained that his spectacles were the wrong prescription and, in spite of frequent changes, he continued to complain about not being able to see clearly.

'Great,' he said.

'Could you read me some of the article?' I ventured.

'Sure,' he smiled, and began to read from a narrow column about a train accident that had happened the previous day on the Edinburgh to Glasgow line. He reached the end, looked up and smiled.

'See, no problem.'

It never ceases to amaze me what I saw Paul do. The column was no more than three centimetres wide, but he had only read the right half of it, down its entire length.

'You read it all?' I asked, tentatively.

'Oh yes – no problem.'

'Do you mind if I ask you what it was about?'

'A train crash,' he said, cheerfully.

'Anything else – can you remember where it was, for instance?'

'Ah you know, just the usual . . .' he said.

Paul had read two or three hundred words that could have been plucked randomly from the dictionary, because he had only read the right half of each short line. But that wasn't what was puzzling me. What was intriguing me was that *he didn't have any awareness that he was reading gobbledygook*! How could this intelligent man, a trained engineer who was highly literate and a good conversationalist, not realize that what he was reading made no sense?

I realized that Paul wasn't checking himself and so just didn't see the contradictions and gaps in his reading. He wasn't, as the jargon has it, 'self-monitoring'.

'Paul, can I ask you to remind me what you think your main problems are now?'

'I'm not bad really – left leg's a bit weak sometimes, but nothing too bad.'

'What about your left arm?' He glanced down at it, hanging limp by the side of his chair, and hoisted it up on to the arm.

'I suppose it's a bit weak sometimes, too, but I manage fine.'

'Any other problems?'

'No, can't say I have.'

'What about your vision?'

'I could do with some new glasses – these ones are a bit blurry sometimes, but they're OK.'

'What about reading?'

'Great, no problem.' This was the same day he 'read' the newspaper for me.

Much later, after many, many visits, if I mentioned his spatial neglect, he would sometimes acknowledge that he might occasionally miss things on his left side, but I got the impression that he might be trying to please me and wasn't really convinced.

He never spontaneously complained about problems with spatial neglect and it was clear to me that mostly he wasn't aware of it, even when he was reading essentially random collections of words. And even when he did, with prompting, mention it, there was an abstract quality to the way he talked about it, as if it was something someone had told him about and not anything personal to him. Spatial neglect wasn't just about paying attention to the left side, I concluded – it was a fundamental problem of *awareness*.

I didn't properly think through Paul's awareness problems at the time and I certainly didn't link them to more general ideas of self-awareness; that is something I regret now, because I was to find out later that self-awareness is a critical ingredient in dealing with stress in a way that builds personal resilience. Instead, twenty years and four cities – Rome, Cambridge, Dublin and New York – later, I eventually came back to the nature of self-awareness and how and why it goes wrong in people like Paul, a topic that, while intriguing, is also complicated and so I will have to come back to it in Chapter 6.

By the time I was seeing Paul I had lost contact with my art friend Sam, but from time to time I did think about him and his theory of rightward kissing. But as I watched Paul constantly veering to the right side of his page, plate and world, it never occurred to me that this had anything to do with what Sam had noticed in the Tate Gallery.

The Kiss *Revisited*

And then, one day, while flicking through the pages of *Nature*, comfortable on the green leather of an armchair in the Senior Common Room at Trinity College Dublin, I sat bolt upright.

'Good God, Sam was right!' I blurted out, drawing some frowns from behind spread newspapers across the hushed, portrait-hung room.

Onur Güntürkün, of the Ruhr University Bochum in Germany, observed 124 kissing couples in airports, railway stations, beaches and parks across the USA, Germany and Turkey.[3] Just as Sam had noticed in his works of art, people kissed to the right twice as often as to the left. Now my curiosity was really piqued – why on earth should this be the case?

The obvious explanation – and the one that Güntürkün opted for – was that this bias just reflected the fact that more people are right-handed. The dominant left brain veers the body rightward for everything, including kisses.

Armed with my knowledge of Rodin's sculpture, however, I didn't quite buy that explanation, although I couldn't say exactly why. Science is funny like that – sometimes I have hunches without being able to fully justify them. I may notice something about a patient – like Paul's strange detachment, for instance – and that connects with a paper I read or a chance remark by a smart colleague like Ken Heilman.

Scientists tend to get hung up on single issues that may seem a bit irrelevant to non-scientists, but they gnaw away at them for years, trying to make sense of them. That's certainly been true for me in trying to understand how it is we manage to keep our mind on boring, routine activities like reading a dull textbook or driving a train down the same track day after day.

Most new ideas in science come from finding out how something *works*, rather than tackling practical problems head on. By understanding better how we sustain our attention, I've not only been able to discover its genetic and biochemical links, and found out how to measure the action of a key neurotransmitter in the living human brain, I have also been able to develop new methods for training people like Christine, Paul and Sally to cope better with their difficulties.

Because attention is key to our mental and emotional life, getting below the skin of just one small aspect of attention can have quite big spin-offs.

But a hunch is just that – a hunch – and the only way to test it out is the lengthy business of gathering data to see whether the ideas are right or wrong. I would estimate that, throughout my career, my hunches have been right about a third of the time and wrong the rest of the time. Given how challenging and time-consuming human research can be, that is a lot of research that goes nowhere, and it can be quite discouraging at times. But when you do make a discovery, the exhilaration is just great, making up for all the grind and the failures along the way.

So, around 1989, when I was working in Italy at the University of Rome, I had a hunch about the Rodin findings and I *think* it may have been all these months watching Paul's left hand in Edinburgh that kindled it. Let me explain: Paul's stroke had left him partially paralysed down his left side. He could walk with great difficulty and only with help, and, though he could move his left arm and hand a little, he tended not to unless you reminded him. He could lift his left hand slightly but couldn't do much with it.

The usual explanation for this sort of lack of spontaneous movement is that their attention is twisted to the right and so they don't focus on the left side of their bodies.

But my hunch was lurking in the background, and, at a conference in Germany, I saw something that brought it out of the shadows of my subconscious. Normally we think movements follow what we pay attention to – after all, attention is king, isn't it? You reach for the cup because you are looking at it. But colleagues in Montreal had discovered that what you *do* can affect your attention just as attention impacts what you do.[4]

They had studied patients with the same problem as Paul's – left spatial neglect – and asked them to point to targets on a screen. Not surprisingly, they missed many targets on the left side – that is, when they used their right hands. But when they did the same search pointing with their *left* hands, their attention to the left got better.

My hunch was slowly changing from a semi-conscious inkling to a conscious hypothesis. Paul couldn't point with his left hand, but he could move it a little. Would making these little movements help to rebalance his attention?

Yes! As Paul moved his left fingers slowly and clumsily up and down under the table while he tried to read, he noticed many more of the words on the left side of the page than normal. But if he crossed his hand over to the right side of his body, moving it there had no effect on his reading. So it wasn't the mere fact of moving the left side of his body – he had to move it on the left of the space surrounding him.[5]

Paul was pleased to help and enjoyed taking part in these studies, though of course he had no inkling what ideas were being tested until after we had finished collecting the data. After many more sessions like these,[6] I was able to boil the results down to this: when Paul made the effort to move his left hand – someone else moving it for him had no effect – it made him attend better to the outside world and miss less on the left side.

I still wasn't clear why, and was no further on in explaining Rodin's *The Kiss*. Then, in scanning Paul's medical notes for clues one day, I noticed something that sparked my interest: in the notes there was an entry that I had written many months before. It said that Paul had 'full visual fields'. This meant that there was nothing wrong with his vision – when he looked straight ahead and I moved a finger of my right hand on the left side of his vision, he saw it immediately and the same for the right.

But I had also written 'left visual extinction' in Paul's notes: this means that when I held up my two hands, one to the left of Paul's vision and one to the right, and moved them both together, he only saw the right finger move. So, while Paul could see something on the left on its own, when there was competition from another movement on the right, he didn't notice the movement on the left.

I hurried to see Paul the next day so that I could test my hunch. As before, when he clumsily moved his left hand, he noticed things on the left side more easily. But what happened when he moved his left and his right hands together? He was back to square one, his attention twisted to the right just as much as before: I had discovered what I called 'motor extinction' – the movement equivalent of visual extinction.[7]

By now, a hunch was beginning to incubate about why Rodin's sculptures kissed to the right.

Visual extinction is evidence that the two halves of the brain are competitors. But when one is damaged – say, by a stroke, like Paul's – then its ability to compete with the other is weakened. When I wiggled my finger on the left side of Paul's vision, he saw the movement because there was nothing on the right to compete with it. But when I wiggled my fingers to both his left and his right, the healthy left half of the brain noticed its finger moving on his right, but snuffed out its rival right hemisphere's ability to notice my finger moving on the left side.

This is 'inhibition' at work, with the two halves of the brain in a constant, usually friendly, struggle to inhibit each other. But that struggle was no longer amicable within Paul's brain after his stroke, because the right half had been weakened. This was 'extinction' at work, but I had discovered something quite new – that extinction affected action as well as perception. This discovery led me to develop a new treatment for spatial neglect that helped Paul and hundreds of other people with similar problems, which I'll come back to later in the chapter.

Could it be that the rightward turning of Rodin's figures and the embracing airport couples had something to do with competition and inhibition between the two halves of the couples' brains?

Goalkeepers, Happy Dogs and Nietzsche

Penalty shootouts following tied football matches are nerve-racking affairs and they tend to happen on big, high-pressure occasions – cup finals, for instance. They are essentially mind games in which football skill plays a comparatively small part. Something which any professional player can do without a thought in training – kick the ball past the goalkeeper's gaping twenty-four-foot-wide goal from a distance of thirty-six feet – becomes mental torture for the penalty taker in front of 60,000 people at the end of a crucial decider.

The goalkeeper has a near-impossible job, too. Unless he can read the penalty taker's mind as to which direction he's going to shoot, it is a matter mostly of chance whether he dives in the correct direction or not. And so it works out under most circumstances that the goalkeeper dives to the right roughly the same number of times as he dives to the left.

But there is one exception to this.

With the two teams taking five alternate shots at goal, the pressure on the goalkeeper who has earlier failed to save builds enormously as he comes up to the final penalty. And it turns out that in these circumstances, when they are behind in the penalty shootout, goalkeepers dive to the right seven times out of ten, and to the left only three times out of ten.[8]

The pressure on the trailing goalkeeper makes him desperate to save the next penalty. The Dutch researchers who discovered this goalkeeper effect argue that being very strongly motivated to act switches on the left side of the brain more than the right. That's why, they argue, the left hemisphere of the goalkeeper's brain dominates the right, biasing him slightly towards the right and so triggering a right dive 70 per cent of the time.

This, I realized, is strangely similar to what happened in Paul's brain, where his healthy left hemisphere dominated the weakened right hemisphere, pushing him to the right, also.

But why should the left side of a highly motivated goalkeeper's brain be more active than the right? I couldn't quite work this out until by chance one day I came across (this is not a joke) a study about tail-wagging in dogs.

It turns out that when dogs see their owners, they not only wag their tails vigorously, but they wag them more to the right than to the left.[9] Show them a cat, and their tails wag less strongly, but still more to the right than to the left. But reveal a strange dog – a fearsome male Belgian Shepherd Malinois, to be specific – and their tail wagging not only declines significantly, but it switches direction and goes more leftward than rightward.

Wanting something means that you are inclined to *approach* it. When we are with someone we like we tend to lean in their direction in what we can think of as a gentle movement, perhaps mildly yearning or straining towards them. This is quite the opposite of what happens when we dislike or fear something or someone, when we tend to draw away and *avoid* it or them, backing off both physically and mentally.

Our physical movements mirror our mental states. One of the fundamental mental states is desire and the inclination to get nearer to the object of our desire. The dogs' desire to approach their owners made their tails wag more to the right because feeling strongly motivated to *approach* something you want depends more on the left frontal lobe of the brain than the right. And one by-product of this increased activity in the left half of the brain is that it spills over into the body and twists it slightly to the right because the left-side movement parts of the brain are also activated more than the right ones.

This also happens to the under-pressure goalkeeper: he badly wants to save the penalty, and this 'wanting' activates the left more than the right half of the brain, which in turn spills over into his brain's control over bodily movements. This results in his body being twisted fractionally more towards the right so that when he makes his reflex dive to save, he is primed to dive more often to the right than to the left.

This, then, explains Rodin's *The Kiss*. During a passionate embrace, you want something – sex – and this desire boosts the activity in the left side of the brain enough to overcome the competition with the right side, leading to a torque towards the right.

The right and left halves of the brain are rivals, competitors, like young brothers constantly engaged in a friendly tussle with each other. But if you fire up the left brother with an emotion-laden goal, he will overcome his right brother, in spite of the latter's attempts to resist this racked-up competition.

In Paul's case, the right brain was weak and injured, and so the left brain could dominate, edging his world to the right just like Rodin's figures. I had managed to redress some of this unfair imbalance by teaching Paul to move his left hand. But he wasn't fired up emotionally – in fact, as I mentioned earlier, he was quite disengaged and certainly wasn't *hungering* after something the way Rodin's figures, the under-pressure goalkeepers or the happy dogs were.

But there *was* a certain relentlessness about Paul: when he was in a wheelchair, he might find himself blocked by a door frame catching the left wheel, but he would just keep trying to push forward, without appearing to stop or consider an alternative to just pressing on. You could see it when he was eating, too, as he kept stabbing away at the empty right side of his plate, oblivious to the fact that the potato he was chasing had skidded over to his neglected left side.

The jargon term for this sort of behaviour is 'perseveration' and Paul showed quite a lot of it. There was a strange inexorability about his pursuit of his goal, oblivious to feedback – a bit like Rodin's figures, absorbed in their passionate embrace.

Except that Paul totally lacked their passion. Why? I remembered Ken Heilman's disturbing photographs and his patients' blunt emotional responses to them, their inertly dry skin which showed no little glint of sweat signifying *arousal*. Paul, unlike Rodin's kissers, had very low levels of arousal: his heart was not beating like a drum, nor was his stomach tightening with desire. All Paul had was this rather nerveless and rightward-veering relentlessness, *going forward* towards whatever goal he had in mind. This relentlessness didn't feel like some Nietzschean determination to overcome difficulties, so I was a bit stuck about where to go from here.

I tend to write in the early morning and one day I had to break off to give a lecture. As I walked along the side of one of Trinity College's exquisite eighteenth-century squares, mulling over what felt like a stalemate in my quest, I found myself stopping dead outside number 39 New Square. I looked up at a plaque there and read that this was Samuel Beckett's former apartment, where the Nobel Prize winner had lived for three years when he was teaching at Trinity. Could I have a possible answer to my problem?

I turned sharply on my heel. With half an hour to go before the lecture, I just had time to run across the square to the Berkeley Library, where I found what I was looking for immediately. My link to Nietzsche. The last words in Beckett's novel *The Unnamable*.[10]

'You must go on, I can't go on, I'll go on.'

I realized that I had a partial answer: it came to me that people who are strengthened by adversity almost always have this capacity for *going on* – that is, keeping going. They don't have lust on their side, as Rodin's figures had; nor are they emotionally blunted by under-arousal like Paul. But there is a relentless quality – a grim determination occasionally laced with gallows humour – which drives them *forwards*.

It came to me that, for Nietzsche's phrase to be true, a person has to be able to take this existential position of 'going on' without even knowing what exactly it is you are going on towards. It is a goal with no content. Or, rather, the goal is itself simply to *go on*. And for Nietzsche's dictum to apply to you, I realized, you just have to *go on* through the darkness of adversity without either knowing what will happen, or expecting anything.

To be able to do this may be the essence of the human spirit.

I was sure that part of the Nietzsche jigsaw was in place. To be strengthened by adversity you have to *approach* life – to go on – without the benefit of passion or reward. You need to use the human brain's remarkable freedom to conjure up out of pure existence an abstract *approach* to life, that is, the ability to *go on*.

But to go on you need to overcome . . . overcome what? Fear, I suppose. But fear of what? Beckett's words again, this time from *Worstward Ho*: 'Ever tried. Ever failed. No matter. Try again. Fail again. Fail better.'[11]

Of course, it is fear of failure that so often holds us back. And at once I understood that if Rodin had created a sculpture about fear rather than about passion, then his figures would likely have been turning leftwards. Just as passion is about *approach and reward*, fear is, I suddenly understood, about *avoidance and punishment*.

That's why the dogs wagged their tails leftwards when faced with the Belgian Shepherd: suddenly they had switched from a joyful approach towards their owners to fearful withdrawal from a threat. For humans, failure is a threat every bit as real as a Belgian Shepherd.

Beckett's *going on*, then, is an act of will, a deliberate switching on of our brain's approach system, a conscious biasing of the brain's left hemisphere to override the anxiety-laden withdrawal of the right.

I knew from my work with Paul and other patients that the two halves of the brains are rivals, constantly trying to inhibit the other. But had I gone too far with this Beckett and tail-wagging? Did Paul's problems really have anything to do with Rodin, goalkeepers and happy dogs?

After all, it's easy for the dog who sees his owner to wag his tail – ancient loyalty creates a powerful emotion which switches on his brain's approach system. And for the goalkeeper, there is the hot breath of 60,000 fans and anxious teammates stoking the fire of his urge to go forward. But if you have just had something bad happening to you, it can be a struggle to find any emotional drivers to make you go on. For a while at least, it's all down to a pure act of determination to *go on*.

But what about Paul? It didn't seem to me that his was an act of will to go on: there was something too 'absent' about his particular style of relentless going forward. True, he veered to the right like the dogs and the goalkeepers, but it was neither animal passion nor Beckett-like determination that drove him. So what was it?

It came to me almost at once: *lack of opposition from his damaged right brain*. In spite of his low levels of alertness and arousal, Paul's brain was in unfettered approach mode because it faced little opposition from the damaged right brain's avoidance tendencies. While the right frontal lobe is associated with caution and inhibition, the left is connected to approach-linked 'go-getter' modes. In the Rodin figures, it was passion and a desire for sex that overwhelmed the caution and inhibition that the right half of the brain is inclined to, driving the statues rightwards. In Paul's case it was just the unfettered go-getter tendencies of the left hemisphere that, unopposed by his damaged right brain, drove him in his emotionally flat, rather bloodless way, *onwards* and, of course, rightwards.

But how relevant Paul's experience was to the wider world was a worry to me. I had invented a way of teaching neglect patients to move their left hands using a simple device that bleeped whenever they hadn't moved them for the last few seconds. This helped them develop the habit of moving their left hands, which in turn helped them to recover a little faster.[12] But I remained unsure about whether Paul's problems really were relevant to how people cope with stress. It took another ten years to be convinced that they were.

In 2012 I wrote a book about power and how it changes people. *The Winner Effect*[13] showed that even remembering a time when you have a little bit of power over someone – like carrying out an annual appraisal on them, for instance – changes the way you think, feel and behave: it makes you more egocentric, uninhibited and smarter, for example.

Remembering a time when *you* were in someone *else's* power – at the receiving end of an appraisal, for example – alters you in a different way, making you less able to solve problems, more sensitive to other people's expressions and generally more wary.

Our environment – and in particular our relationships with other people – can change us completely, from our psychology to the chemistry of our brains. Power raises testosterone in both men and women, and this in turn chemically changes the brain by increasing the activity of the chemical messenger dopamine.

This, then, was a new departure for me, into a new area called social neuroscience, where in fact I hadn't published any original research of my own. I was very surprised then, to discover that in fact, power *is* linked to my research on attention and the tussle between the left and right sides of our brains.

David Wilkinson and his colleagues at the University of Kent found that if you make people feel powerless, it twists their attention leftward – the same direction as the fearful dogs facing the big Belgian Shepherd wagged their tails and the opposite way to the direction the goalkeepers dived.[14]

Wilkinson's participants were first made to feel powerless by remembering a time when someone had power over them. Then they were asked to carry a laden tray down a very narrow corridor. Because their attention was turned leftward by the feeling of powerlessness, their trays bumped off the right wall more often than when they did not feel powerless. Their right frontal lobe's avoidance-inducing activity had been boosted, meaning they paid more attention to the left side of their bodies and less attention to the right. This boosted right brain activity also inhibited their left brain's activity, leading to more collisions with the right wall.

This is exactly the opposite of Paul, who was forever bumping into doorways and objects on his *left* side. Something was boosting the right brain activity of the healthy young tray carriers in the Wilkinson power study, causing it to inhibit their left brains and push them leftwards. That something was a memory of feeling powerless.

Then I found another piece of research looking more directly at what happened in the brain when people were made to feel powerful by writing about a time when they had power over someone. Exactly in line with the tray-walking study, activity in the left frontal lobe of the brain increased when people were made to feel powerful.[15]

When someone has power over you, *going forward* is often not an option, because you don't control your own goals – the power holder does. You can decide that you want to do x or y, but your boss/parent/big brother/teacher/bully/appraiser/partner has the power to override your decision. Rather than making you *approach* your future goals, powerlessness tends to *inhibit* you while you wait to see what the power holder decides for you.

The right front part of the brain has a particular job to do in inhibiting other parts of the brain.[16] Suppose, for instance, you are talking to someone at a party and you begin to make a jokey, mildly mocking comment about a colleague when suddenly you remember that the person you are talking to is friendly with the colleague. You jam on your mental brakes and catch yourself before you say what your brain was preparing to say. This is *inhibition* at work, and the right frontal lobe of your brain is part of your brain's brake system.

Think of when you get an unexpected fright. What do you do? You *freeze*. This is the brain inhibiting normal activity while it scans for threat. The right frontal lobe of the brain is specialized for this sort of *withdrawal* from everyday goals – it avoids, in other words. Being in someone else's power is potentially threatening and can be a source of uncertainty and even fear. This is why lacking power switches on the right brain avoidance system, a consequence of which is that the left brain's approach system is inhibited.

The tug-of-war between approach and avoidance is a fundamental feature – perhaps *the* fundamental feature of our day-to-day lives. *Will I, won't I? Will I say yes to him or no? Will I leave this job or not? Will I buy this car or not? Will I go for that scan or not?* Goals are about seeking *rewards* – a new relationship, a new job, a new car – which make us go forward. But avoidance is all about trying to evade *punishment* – rejection, bad debt, cancer.

Rewards and punishments are the primitive push-pull drivers of all animals, including humans. This was the insight of the great English psychologist Jeffrey Gray, who proposed that every human being is the protagonist in a perpetual struggle between reward/approach and punishment/avoidance.[17] So fundamental are these drivers to our survival that we have evolved two brain systems, one more left-localized in the brain and oriented towards *approach* while the other is more right-localized and tending to *avoid*.[18] As I thought about these discoveries, my mind wandered to one of my earliest cases as a clinical psychologist – a young woman called Gloria who I saw in London in 1976.

Gloria

Some people spend a lifetime in avoidance mode. I remembered Gloria, a thirty-year-old researcher at a university in the south of England who came to see me because of severe anxiety. When I asked her how long it had lasted, she paused for a long few seconds, then said in a thin, choking voice, 'All my life.'

'I can't remember a day in my life when I didn't wake up feeling frightened,' she sobbed the first time I saw her. I couldn't find any particular trauma in her background and she had good relationships with her parents, though a rather tense and uncomfortable one with her younger, much more outgoing and confident sister. Her mother had always been very shy and Gloria believed that she had inherited this shyness in magnified form:

'School was torture – I couldn't wait to get back home every day.'

Lonely and isolated, Gloria felt anxious even about opening a letter:

'I don't know, it's silly . . . but I get this sense of dread when a letter comes for me – it's like it's going to be something bad, like I'm sacked, or have some terrible illness . . . or have done something terrible to hurt someone . . .'

Gloria's mind was primed to expect *punishment.*

She had a couple of close friends from childhood, but generally as far as she was concerned other people were walking powder kegs of potential disapproval or rejection.

'My friends have sort of moved on – they got fed up asking me to go out with them and I was always cancelling at the last minute, so they don't bother asking me any more.'

Interviews were a torture and her blushing, tongue-tied performance put off all but the most perceptive of potential employers.

'I knew I could do the job, but sitting there, three of them behind the desk, looking at me – I just clammed up, could only answer *yes* or *no*. When they asked me if I had any questions, I couldn't think of any – my mind was a blank, and I just ran out.'

Gloria was very bright indeed and exceptionally good at her job – providing, that is, she didn't have to work too closely with other people.

Gloria also constantly suffered from colds and chest infections because her immune system was taking such a battering from the chronic anxiety: chronic stress degrades the immune system and makes it less able to fight off infections. Her sex life had been very limited and, though she was quite pretty, she shied away from men, avoiding the potential uncertainty and threat which they, like most other people, presented.

I was still training as a clinical psychologist at the time I saw Gloria and had been well prepared to deal with phobias and obsessive-compulsive disorders, but there was nothing I had yet learned – this was shortly before the CBT revolution was to hit our profession – that could help me understand or treat someone with such general anxiety and avoidance. Gloria had been given anti-anxiety drugs by her family doctor, and then antidepressants by the psychiatrist who referred her to me, but to little effect. The best I could do was to teach her a type of progressive muscular relaxation which helped tone down the anxiety and let her sleep a little better, but did not stop her constant, gnawing anxiety and avoidance of so much in life.

Lurking behind her anxiety was that painful self-consciousness that so many of my anxious patients showed so much, like Simon and Lucy, or so little, like Paul. Gloria would become inarticulate in interviews because, rather than thinking about the question and how she'd answer it, she would listen to herself speak, feeling the hot flush on her cheeks and scanning the interviewers' faces for signs of disapproval. Little wonder she found it so hard to get jobs.

Gloria had spent a lifetime with her brain stuck in avoidant mode. In Jeffrey Gray's terms, her 'Behavioural Inhibition System' was dominating her mind, making her constantly vigilant for threat, overanxious, overcautious, easily startled, constricted in her movements, eyes darting, head bowed, a little stooped and, above all, excruciatingly self-conscious.

I knew nothing at the time about Gray's so-called 'Behavioural Inhibition System' and its rival 'Behavioural Activation System', nor that Gloria's overactive right frontal lobe may have been suppressing its left counterpart into lowered activity. Gloria was so filled with fears about the bad things that might happen to her that she found it impossible to contemplate the good things that she might look forward to with the help of her brain's approach network.

'If I think about meeting a friend – Sylvia, say – as soon as I start thinking about it being nice to meet her, it's like my mind starts throwing up all these things that could go wrong – she won't turn up, I'll have a migraine and will leave her waiting, the trains will be cancelled and I won't be able to get home . . . so I don't even try to arrange stuff.'

The same applied to her career. Gloria knew she was very bright and very good at what she did, and somewhere inside her there was a deep ambition. But she couldn't translate that ambition into goals that would advance it – like presenting a paper at a conference or applying for a job in another university. The moment she imagined herself achieving something like that – and hence enjoying feelings of empowerment and achievement – her overactive avoidance system would quickly shut down the approach-related anticipation and replace positive, exciting and happy thoughts with dismal, anxiety-filled images of defeat, threat and rejection.

'I know it sounds stupid – my boss says it is. She says my work is really good, but that I need to get it out there . . . but I keep thinking it's not really good enough and not finished so I can't submit it to the conference or the journal.'

I discovered, alas many years too late for me to be of help to Gloria, that the fact that her approach and avoidance systems were out of balance probably changed Gloria's brain chemistry. Had she been able to set a goal for herself and achieve it, her brain's *reward network*, which is to be found deep in the middle of the brain, would have been activated, which would have led to the release of higher levels of the chemical messenger dopamine. Dopamine is a 'feel-good' neurotransmitter – a chemical messenger in the brain – which fuels the brain's response to reward and hence boosts the approach system.

As I tried to reconstruct Gloria's problems with the benefit of hindsight from my newly discovered perspective of right-left, approach-avoidance, I found that indeed there is evidence for more dopamine involvement in left brain function,[19,20] while the alertness chemical messenger which I described in Chapter 1, noradrenaline, is more strongly linked to right brain function.[21] Gloria, I suspected, had less dopamine activity in the left frontal parts of her brain than her more confident, approach- and reward-focused friends. And she certainly was constantly in a more alert and anxious state, always worrying about possible downsides – punishments – and so with higher than normal levels of noradrenaline.

In the mid-1990s, after I moved to Cambridge from Edinburgh, I had some doubts about this left-right, approach-avoidance story, however. Much of it is based on correlational studies, and correlations don't prove cause and effect. There has been a lot of research which has found that people who show more approach in their behaviour have higher left frontal lobe activity, while those who tend towards avoidance have more right hemisphere activity.[22] And there is also evidence to show that people who are more reward- and approach-focused had more receptors – receiving stations – for dopamine in the left side of their brains than the right.[23]

My doubts lingered on for a decade until in 2013 a study was published which clinched it for me.[24] These Harvard researchers assembled a group of students who were polar opposites to Gloria – they were reward-hungry, approach-oriented go-getters who weren't overtroubled by what other people thought of them and were willing to take a chance on any new opportunity.

Not surprisingly, these students had much higher activity in the left frontal lobes of their brains than was the case for their less approach-oriented fellow students.

But, did this have anything to do with dopamine? The researchers answered this question by giving the students a short-acting 'dopamine antagonist' – a drug that reduces dopamine activity in the brain. What happened? The left frontal lobe activity bombed, while the right frontal activity began to dominate.

I was reassured: this wasn't a random correlation. Approach, dopamine and the left frontal lobe hung together, as did avoidance, noradrenaline and the right frontal lobe. If we had had this sort of brain imaging in 1976, Gloria's right frontal lobe would have been very, very active, I guessed.

But it was another piece of research that really brought home to me what had lain at the heart of Gloria's difficulties.

Students in Toronto were asked to quickly summarize a passage about statistical methods in less than two minutes; they were told that the topic was standard knowledge in their field. Unknown to the students, however, half of them read a passage that didn't make sense, while the other half summarized a clear, comprehensible passage.[25]

The time pressure and the impossibility of the task given to the first group made them feel uncertain, frustrated and confused – they found it, in other words, very threatening. So, here was the key question – how did they react to *their* threat?

Gloria lived in a world of more or less continuous threat. Her right frontal lobe would have been chronically active, I believed, because of her avoidant stance towards that threat. In the Toronto study, then, the students who felt threatened by the impossible task should have increased their right frontal lobe activity as they retreated from the threat.

And, yes, some of the students did show a small increase in the activity on the right side of their brains.

But another group didn't . . . in fact, this group showed a massive increase in *left* brain activity. Who were these two groups of people?

Take a moment to think how you would answer these questions.

'I can do things as well as most other people.'

'I feel I have quite a lot to be proud of.'

'I take a positive attitude towards myself.'

The more you answer *no* to questions like these, the lower is your *self-esteem*.

It was the students with *low* self-esteem whose brains reacted to threat in the way I thought Gloria's would have – by increasing right brain, avoidance, activity. But the high self-esteem students showed a dramatically opposite pattern – their left frontal lobe activity shot up, showing that they were *approaching* or confronting the threat. You need to *respect yourself*, I had learned, if you are to benefit from stress through your brain rising to challenge rather than shrinking from threat.

I puzzled how I might have helped Gloria had I known all this thirty years ago. How could I have helped her to escape from the paralysis of avoidance, withdrawal and fear of punishment? My psychiatry colleagues assumed that only drugs could help her, even though none had so far. And my training hadn't equipped me to treat such widespread anxiety.

Except that it had.

The Institute of Psychiatry in London, where I trained, was the home of 'behaviourism' in Europe, led by the world-famous psychologist Hans Eysenck. We learned to treat problems that patients had as 'behaviours', with the assumption that if you managed to help someone change their behaviour, then the feelings linked to that behaviour would change, too.

Behaviourism had its philosophical and practical limitations, and was much criticized at the time for ignoring people's subjective mental worlds and the role of unobservable thoughts and emotional processes in shaping their actions. It was largely overtaken by cognitive psychology, and in the applied, clinical world, by cognitive behaviour therapy – CBT – which rightly recognized the role of people's thoughts and beliefs in shaping how they felt and behaved.

I trained myself in CBT during the late 1970s, because a purely behavioural training had left me ill-equipped to help many of the patients I was asked to see when I moved to Scotland to take up my first job there in 1978. But over the next three decades I saw psychologists come to neglect the 'behavioural' part of CBT in favour of a very big focus on the 'cognitive' part – namely, largely talking therapy aimed at identifying and changing thinking patterns underlying emotional problems. I was no exception to this trend.

This was a real pity, because by the 1990s research was emerging showing that not only did our thoughts affect our emotions, but so did our *actions*. New research appeared in the 1990s showing that not only is how you behave affected by your emotions, but the opposite was also true – what you *do* affects how you *feel*.[26]

The classic demonstration of this is to ask some people to hold a pencil between their clenched teeth, which forces the lips into an artificial smile. Others have to hold the pencil between their pursed lips, which forces their mouth into an artificial scowl. Even though no one knows what the purpose is of what they are doing, the fake smile people rate themselves as significantly happier than those with the fake scowl.[27]

The idea that what we do controls how we feel was far from new. In fact, at the Maudsley Hospital in London we were exceptionally well trained in using behavioural treatments to treat problems such as phobias. These purely behavioural treatments work very well with straightforward phobias most of the time.

A typical patient of mine at the time was a woman – Jill – who was completely incapacitated by a phobia of snakes, in spite of the fact that there were no snakes in south London. She had lived in Africa for a few years where she had encountered snakes once or twice, but this fear had incubated and expanded on her return home, to the extent that, if she caught a glimpse of a lamp flex out of the corner of her eye, she would be seized with panic. Since she had learned that she might be moving back to Africa for work reasons, her phobia was becoming a real problem and was filling her mind in the same way my adolescent mind had been filled with the terror of the piping party.

The main type of behavioural treatment we learned was called 'graded exposure'. This means what it sounds like – gradually exposing people to the things that frighten them, while steadily increasing the fearfulness or closeness of the items. Having thoroughly interviewed Jill and her husband to check that this was indeed a straightforward phobia and not a more complicated psychological problem, I explained to her the rationale and methods of graded exposure and behaviour therapy.

Then together we created a 'fear ladder' – a series of situations that ranged from the mildly frightening up to panic-inducing terror. Jill ordered the rungs on the ladder according to how frightening she thought it would be. Here was her ladder, along with her 0–100 fear rating for each item.

- Stay for thirty minutes in a strange room which has several power cords 'snaking' under furniture. 20/100
- Stay for thirty minutes in a room with both power cords and pieces of rope 'snaking' under furniture. 25/100
- Look at photographs of snakes. 30/100
- Reach into a closed bag in which there are coils of cord and rope. 35/100
- Look at a relatively unrealistic toy snake on the table in front of you. 40/100
- Handle the toy snake for at least two minutes. 50/100
- Look at a very realistic model snake. 55/100
- Handle the realistic snake for at least two minutes. 60/100
- Stay in the Zoo reptile house with the snakes behind the glass for five minutes. 70/100
- Stay in the room with a live snake on the table ten feet away for at least five minutes. 80/100
- Stay in the room with a live snake on the table five feet away for at least five minutes. 85/100
- Stay in the room with a live snake on the table two feet away for at least five minutes. 90/100
- Touch the live snake. 95/100
- Pick up the live snake. 100/100

Jill got through the first two items in a matter of minutes in our first treatment session. Faced with the photos, it took a little longer for her to get used to them, but by the end of the first session she could look at them without anxiety. The jargon for this process is 'habituation', where the brain's emotional system gradually stops responding to a stimulus that appears again and again without something bad happening.

We then moved on to the fourth step in the ladder – handling the ropes and cords in a closed bag. She became very anxious and stressed at this stage, and needed a lot of reassurance to do it a second time, then a third. But by the time she had done this a dozen times, she had no anxiety. We then moved on to the toy snakes – this again wasn't easy for her, but she habituated, though the *very* realistic python I had bought in the shop at London Zoo took her an entire hour before she became so comfortable with it that she was able to drape it round her neck.

She dreaded the visit to the reptile house at London Zoo and she was an ashen, drawn figure when I met her there one foggy February morning, by special arrangement with the Zoo outside of opening hours. But, two hours later, I had left her in there on her own and she was, reasonably happily, wandering about and looking at the various snakes.

The final session, with a live snake, took place in the back room of a local pet shop. We were in there for more than an hour, Jill's anxiety levels hitting the ceiling at first. But then, step by step, she moved up the last five rungs of her fear ladder, until, finally, she touched the snake.

She never managed to bring herself to pick it up, but that didn't matter – her phobia was 95 per cent vanquished and her mind freed from its torturing anxiety. Jill was to all intents and purposes 'cured'. She still didn't like snakes, but she knew that in reality there was very little chance of meeting one in the city where she would be working.

Anxiety about a simple thing can cause chaos in your life and create real distress – as I had discovered in the Sea Scouts – and it is a most remarkable thing to see how, sometimes, just a simple change can have dramatic changes on a person's whole life. That was true for me when I didn't have to blow the pipe any more, and it was also true for Jill now that her fertile imagination wasn't haunted by the fear of snakes.

Jill felt a surge of confidence and pleasure at achieving the goals of her fear ladder. One of the less recognized consequences of overcoming your fears in a behavioural treatment like this is the fact that achieving success boosts activity in the brain's 'reward network', or 'pleasure centre' as it used to be known. This activity is linked to increased levels of the chemical messenger dopamine, and a biochemical consequence of this is to reduce anxiety. Experiencing success, in other words, can be a little like taking a tranquillizer and an energy drink combined.

In Jill's case, a result of this was to strengthen her brain's approach system against her avoidance tendencies, which because of the phobia had been ruling her life for a long time before I saw her. The more Jill mastered challenges on her fear ladder, the more readily did she take on the next challenge, in spite of her anxiety. Each time she mastered her fear, she felt an exhilaration that reflected the boosted dopamine activity in her brain's reward network – and which strengthened her approach system.

Gloria's problems, however, were more deep-seated than Jill's, and hers was not an isolated phobia in an otherwise reasonably well-adjusted life. Hence I didn't have the success with her that I did with Jill. But had I known what I know now, I think I could have helped Gloria much more than I did. My training had made me focus on her avoidance – on trying to control her anxiety with relaxation training. That was fine as far as it went, but what I should also have done was something I learned many years later from the Dublin-based clinical psychologist Fiona O'Doherty. If I had set very small, achievable goals for Gloria, this would have boosted her self-confidence, and simultaneously given her brain mini-infusions of dopamine which would have diminished her anxiety and avoidance slightly.

The goals could have been tiny, I learned from O'Doherty: go into the common room at coffee time, for instance, and stay there for thirty seconds. Then I could have got Gloria to take her own attention off herself for that half-minute by scanning the room to look for anyone who looked preoccupied or sad. Then leave. It may sound trivial, but for someone like Gloria that would have been an enormous achievement and would have given her a very unfamiliar feeling – of success, achievement . . . even momentary happiness. Such tiny achievements can be built on bit by bit, and Gloria could perhaps have wrested control from the avoidance system in favour of a more positive, approach-oriented outlook on life.

These, I suddenly understood, were part of the way in which, by taking small steps towards mastering a difficulty, we become stronger. The bigger the challenge mastered, the stronger we become. And the mechanics of this lie in the way these small success experiences energize us via the brain's dopamine-linked reward system. And this in turn makes us better able to face up to the next challenge.

People who are dominated by the avoidance system tend to be less happy than those in whom the approach system has the upper hand. They may also be more conscientious and careful, but that's because the prospect of punishment is usually uppermost in their minds. I thought about Gloria's life and her problems. She had suffered no major deprivation or trauma that I could find – no abuse, neglect, illness or injury, nor any psychic trauma – no awful distortions in her early relationships as far as I could tell. Yes, she had a slightly difficult relationship with her sister, but that is far from rare, and she was adamant that it wasn't a source of major stress for her.

How come Gloria suffered like this? It was only when I came across the work of American psychologist Richard Davidson[28] that I could make sense of it. Davidson had taken Jeffrey Gray's approach/avoidance systems and applied them to emotional problems, showing that people with more activity in the left frontal lobe of their brains showed more approach, reward-oriented behaviours, and hence higher mood with less anxiety and depression. Right-frontal-dominant people, on the other hand, tended more to an avoidance mode and consequently suffered lower moods and more anxiety. Remarkably, you can even see this playing out in infants.

Babies of nine to ten months who become more distressed when separated from their mothers for less than a minute, and who are more fearful of strangers, show more activity in the right front part of their brains than babies who show less distress.[29] What's more, in infants as young as six months, those whose right frontal lobes are more active have higher levels of the stress hormone cortisol in their blood.[30] This goes on through childhood and right into adulthood, with many people, like Gloria, enduring chronic fearfulness, worry and withdrawal.[31] Such people tend to be shy and inhibited and wary of unfamiliar situations and people – just like they probably were as infants.

Does this then mean that people like Gloria are doomed to irrevocable anxiety because of an inherited imbalance between the left approach and right avoidance sides of their brains? No. This approach-avoidance balance is an ongoing struggle between the two parts of the brain. True, the more one side dominates, the more it will continue to dominate because its opponent is progressively weakened by a stronger competitor. But just as Paul, whose avoidant side had been damaged by a stroke, learned to redress the right-left balance in his brain using the limited movement of his left hand, surely this should also be possible for people like Gloria?

I came to the conclusion that there was no great Freudian drama to be uncovered in Gloria's unconscious, or any dramatic early experiences to be disentangled, at least as far as I could tell in my many conversations with her. I have seen patients in whom this *was* the case, but Gloria wasn't one of them. Gloria had been a temperamentally anxious infant. Who knows what the reason for that was – it may have been related to the nature of her attachment to her mother, but it could equally well have been a genetically endowed trait in the brain make-up she was born with.

But what had happened throughout her childhood and right into adulthood was that this temperamental tendency to be nervous about new things and shy of strangers kindled a habitually avoidant style that steadily diminished her inclination to approach new situations and new people. And the less she approached the more she avoided, resulting in a vicious circle of increasing anxiety combined with less and less confidence-inspiring approach activity and its energizing, tranquillizing, dopamine-fuelled success experiences. The more she avoided new or challenging situations, the less she exercised her left frontal approach system and so she progressively weakened it. She had, in other words, spent a lifetime in *retreat*.

Gloria had therefore suffered a continual and disabling series of mini-traumas throughout her life. She agonized for days in a state of sleepless, migraine-tortured, heart-pounding, dry-mouthed anxiety before meeting a stranger. Hers was a bit like my rather silly anxiety about piping up the flag in the Sea Scouts writ large. But the difference was that, while my anxiety lasted a few months, her much more severe version haunted her for a lifetime.

So why couldn't Gloria have been strengthened by this adversity? After all, it hadn't killed her. As I had discovered when walking to my lecture through New Square, Trinity, a Beckett-like *going on* has to be part of the answer; otherwise, after a bad experience, your brain would drive you into avoidance, and so cut you off from new rewards and fresh goals.

What I now understood, having thought about Gloria in this context, was that adversity can, in some circumstances, tilt the balance between approach and avoidance and create a vicious cycle of increasingly anxious avoidance which further inhibits the capacity for any kind of approach. This leads to a mind like Gloria's, fixated on future and past punishment and cut off from the possibilities of future reward.

I was making progress. To be strengthened by bad experiences, you don't just have to *go on*, you also have to *retreat less*. But how do you do that?

One way is to reduce the anxiety which is part of avoidance. That is what I was trying to do with Gloria when I taught her to relax her body. It helped her, but only a little. As I was to find out, mastering avoidance and its attendant anxiety is one of the biggest challenges in psychology, which I'll return to in the next chapter.

Was there anything else that might have helped Gloria? It may seem silly, but given the avoidance–left brain link, what about trying what had helped Paul to equal up the competition between the two sides of *his* brain – simple hand movements?

It turned out that someone already had tried this – and it can work.

Gently squeezing a rubber ball in your right hand for a few minutes, for instance, can make you more positive and put you in 'approach mode' by boosting the activity in the left front part of your brain.[32,33] Of course, in Gloria's case this probably wouldn't have made a major difference on its own – but it might have helped by giving her a tiny, temporary boost in confidence before a real challenge such as meeting a stranger.

Another related approach is 'Fake it 'til you make it' – i.e. take a confident 'power pose' (head up, arms spread in a relaxed, space-occupying position) even if you feel terrified inside. Holding such a pose even for a minute or two boosts dopamine activity in your brain because it raises testosterone levels – and this is true for both men *and* women.[34] These chemical changes in your brain make you feel more confident and 'in charge' and so less likely to anxiously avoid a threatening situation.

I use these methods myself if I am feeling anxious about something. For instance, at a TEDx talk in Dublin in 2012 (https://www.youtube.com/watch?v=BdnoqcrTvoc) I was anxiously pacing backstage, anticipating going in front of the biggest audience of my life, some 2,000 people, when my phone buzzed. It was an SMS from my son Niall, saying, 'I hope you're doing your power pose.' It simply hadn't occurred to me. So I snapped into full strutting mode, head back, arms spread and right fist clenched. Pure anecdote, of course, but I strode on to the stage and gave a nerveless performance thanks to my son's timely SMS reminder.

It would have taken much more than a bit of fist-clenching or posture faking to help Gloria to overcome a lifetime of a brain dominated by avoidance, but I am pretty sure that using some of these methods together – setting herself small, achievable goals and boosting her approach to such goals through confident postures and the squeezing of her right fist – could have helped her much more than I was able to do at the time.

Thirty Years On

So where had this thirty-year investigation taken me? Regret that I had not been a better clinical psychologist for Gloria, for one thing – and the surprising discovery that my friend Sam's observation about Rodin's *The Kiss* actually had some scientific basis. But what most struck me was the fact that the competition between the two sides of the brain had such wide ramifications for all the big things in life – our motivations, needs, fears, passion, courage, grit . . . and many more.

I felt that I had partly answered my question about Nietzsche. If 'what doesn't kill me, strengthens me' is to apply, I concluded, first you have to embrace Samuel Beckett's *going on*, however bloodlessly, however empty of emotional impulse. Second, if you are going to allow your brain to rise to tough challenges, you must respect yourself, as the research on self-esteem I described above showed.[35] And thirdly, you must try not to be sucked into a self-perpetuating avoidance mode because that will feed on itself by lessening your inclination to *approach* the future . . . and to *go on*.

But, important as they are, these insights still don't fully address Nietzsche's maxim. They are insufficient because, in thinking about people I have encountered over the years – friends and acquaintances as well as patients – there are some who, despite doing the things that I think make you resilient to stress – going on, respecting themselves, keeping their anxiety in check, etc. – have not been made stronger by adversity. And in a few tragic cases, quite the reverse happened.

So where was I to go next in my search to solve a problem which had become much more complex than I had imagined when I started? I needed to go back to my undergraduate psychology textbooks – and a swinging footbridge in western Canada.

4

Sex and the Suspension Bridge

The Capilano Suspension Bridge over the Capilano River in North Vancouver wobbles and sways as you cross its 450-foot span on flimsy, five-foot-wide wooden struts attached to swinging wire cables. As you gingerly edge across it, all too aware that the wire handrails are much too low to hold you if you stumble, the river surges 230 feet below you in a deep canyon.

This was the scene for one of psychology's famous experiments, carried out in 1974.[1] Stationed on the bridge was an attractive female research assistant who stopped passing men and asked if they would answer some questions for a psychology study of the effects of scenic attractions on creativity. They were asked to write a short story.

The same woman then also stopped male passers-by on a bridge upriver that was solid and unswaying and asked them the same questions. The researchers discovered that the stories written by the swaying bridge men were packed with a sexual content that was completely lacking in the solid bridge stories. What's more, the swaying bridge men were much more likely to try to make personal contact with the research assistant after the study than the solid bridge ones.

I have known vaguely about this research for most of my career. And though there have been some criticisms of its methodology, when I dug into more recent similar research I became convinced that the Capilano Suspension Bridge results were not a fluke.[2]

For example, at a Texas fairground psychologists had roller-coaster riders rate how attracted they were to opposite-sex photo portraits before and after the ride. The flush of fear as they stepped unsteadily from the ride sweetened the attractive-ness of the strangers – or 'love at first fright', as the authors called it.[3]

In trying to work out if and how stress can make you stronger during these past three decades, I have never made any link between that and the swinging bridge study. Gradually, however, I started to look more deeply into what lies behind it.

My first thought was that the fear you are likely to feel on a high, swaying bridge might be an aphrodisiac – perhaps releas-ing a sexual energy fuelling a primitive, life-affirming response to a mortal threat. But what I knew about the effects of stress and anxiety didn't square with that view: on the contrary, fear tends to *inhibit* sexuality via the stress hormone cortisol. It triggers the 'fight or flight' response resulting in beating heart, rapid breathing, pale and sweating skin, and churning stomach.

These responses are all designed to help you survive – hearts race and lungs heave so that there is plenty of oxygen in your arms and legs, blood drains from the outside skin to give fuel to your leg muscles, digestion gets put on hold and there is a deep primal impulse to expel the contents of your bladder and bowel to give you less weight and hence more mobility.

And one other bodily function gets put on hold, too – sex. Sexual fulfilment is not a priority when survival is in question, so fear also dampens down sexual activity and sexual function in a major way. Few things can eliminate a man's erection more quickly than a severe fright and both men's and women's sexual hormone levels are turned down by stress.[4,5]

So, fear is not itself an aphrodisiac: how to explain the swinging bridge findings? Then I remembered – indeed, how could I have forgotten? – one of the very first papers I read when I began to study psychology, a 1962 classic by Stanley Schachter of Columbia University and Jerome Singer titled 'Cognitive, social, and physiological determinants of emotional state'.[6]

These researchers injected either adrenaline or a placebo into volunteers who were left in a waiting room with either a good-natured, joyful companion who joked and played around or an angry, disgruntled person who complained and angrily tore up the lengthy questionnaires they had been asked to complete.

Some of those who were injected with adrenaline were told the symptoms to expect – shaky hands, pounding heart, quicker breathing and flushed-feeling face. They had an explanation for their symptoms – an injected drug. But others were told to expect quite different – wrong – symptoms, including numbness in their feet and itching. These people *didn't* have an explanation for the adrenaline-induced symptoms that would come on after a few minutes.

And it was this latter group, with these unexplained symptoms, who were affected by what the other person in the waiting room – in reality, an actor stooge of the researcher – was doing. The ones who had a happy, contented companion said that they felt happy and excited, while the people with the angry, complaining neighbour said that they felt angry.

What this famous study showed was this: many different emotions have similar bodily symptoms. When we are angry, our pulses race, we breathe faster, we feel our faces flush and our skin becomes sweaty, but when we are happily excited we also breathe faster, feel our faces flush and our skin becomes sweaty. And other emotions cause these general symptoms of increased adrenaline, too – including fear and sexual arousal.

Standing on a swinging bridge, then, doesn't in itself make people sexually aroused. What standing on that fragile, swaying structure high above the torrent *does* do is to make people feel a little frightened. The fear then increases adrenaline – just as Schachter and Singer's injection did – which in turn causes these general symptoms of arousal, racing pulse, fast breathing, etc.

The question now is – how do our minds *interpret* these sensations? The answer from that classic 1962 study is clear: my mind uses the *context* to explain the symptoms to itself. In the case of the young men speaking to an attractive female on the bridge, the context is an attractive girl. So, the men on the bridge, feeling their racing pulses, churning stomachs and sweaty skin, look to the context to make sense of them. And that context is an attractive female showing a personal interest in them, which leads them to think something like 'hey, I'm feeling excited – I'm really attracted to her'.

The old joke about two psychiatrists meeting on the street and one saying to the other 'How am I feeling?' isn't so far off the mark when it comes to how our emotions work. Our minds ask that question of our bodies all the time. But because bodily feelings are so similar across different emotions, we often don't get a clear answer and so have to deduce the emotion from the context.

This helped me understand something else about stress and resilience: how you *interpret* the symptoms of stress can have a big effect on how stressed you actually become.

Mark

Mark was a security guard, or at least he had been until a robber trying to enter the factory he was guarding beat him savagely with an iron bar. Mark had taken early retirement on medical grounds and though eventually he got over his physical injuries, by the time I saw him, two years later, he was not in a good psychological state. Mark's marriage had broken down and he had not been able to hold down a job since leaving the security firm. He was forty-five and his life was not in good shape.

Mark still had some problems with his back, but that was not why his doctor had sent him to me. That said, when he came to see me the first time it was hard for him to pinpoint exactly what was bothering him. He claimed to have got over the injury and moved on, shrugging when I asked him about his feelings about the man who had attacked him: 'He's in and out of prison' was the most I could get out of Mark initially.

Then, suddenly, he began talking about something that had happened earlier that day, on his way to our appointment. The bus he had taken was crowded and he had stood up to give his seat to a pregnant woman. Then a frail old man got on, but no one stood up to give him a seat, not even a teenage girl who was sitting right beside the elderly man.

I was struck by how tense Mark suddenly looked. He had seemed morose, offhand and detached when he first came in, but now he was hunched forward, lips pursed and breathing hard. I glanced at his clenched fists and saw his anger for the first time.

'That girl made you very angry?' I ventured.

He nodded, sitting back a little, as if catching himself.

'How come?'

He shook his head. 'She just sat there – the old guy had to hold on with both hands to stop himself falling over. It just made me so angry!'

'Did you say anything to her?'

'No, I couldn't trust myself not to shout. And there were all these other people just sitting there . . .'

'It sounds like it's hard to get out of your mind.'

He gave a sour smile.

'Round and round like a broken record – I'll wake up in the middle of the night grinding my teeth thinking about her.'

'Does this happen often?'

'Every bloody – sorry about the language – day! Sometimes several times in a day.'

'When was the last time something made you feel like this?'

He laughed sardonically.

'You're not going to believe this – this morning, just after I left the house to come here. I live on a one-way street and this young lad who couldn't have been more than fourteen came riding the wrong way down the street on his push-bike. I had to stop myself running after him. That set me off – I'll be waking up tonight with my heart beating like a drum thinking of him, too.'

He then began to reel off some of the other incidents which plagued his thoughts: a motorcyclist passing through a red light at a pedestrian crossing; someone pushing into a shop queue he was not even standing in; able-bodied people parking in disabled parking spots; others dropping litter on the street; a woman smoking in a no-smoking zone . . . and so on and on in a self-inflicted torture chamber of ruminations which filled Mark's waking life and destroyed his sleep.

It was this relentless, often choking anger that drove him to think about killing himself. He felt that there was no escape from it. And every day threw up new incidents to add to his gallery of rage-provoking vignettes.

I couldn't quite get it – or him – and what it was about all these largely trivial and common, everyday incidents that made him so angry. I feared for Mark's physical health because of the constant pressure of unexpressed anger. What was going on here? I wondered.

And then, one day, it came to me.

'It's when people break the rules.'

He looked at me blankly.

'You get angry when you see people not following rules – like giving up their seat to an old man, or going the wrong way down a one-way street?'

He nodded slowly, then frowned.

'But why do I feel so angry, and why can't I get it out of my mind?' he said faintly. Suddenly he looked exhausted and hopeless.

'Maybe seeing people breaking little rules means that they can break big ones, too?'

He looked at me quizzically.

'I don't get you.'

'. . . like trying to beat a security guard to death?'

He sat back. It was the first time I had seen him relax out of his hunched and angry posture.

'Every time someone breaks a rule it makes you feel that the world is dangerous.'

'Yeah,' he sighed, slumping further into his chair.

Soon after I first met him, Mark had told me what it felt like to be lying on the cold, wet road, his body already broken by the first attack, and to watch with disbelief as the big man standing over him lifted the bar once more, seeing it arc down to an excruciating thud on his leg and the crack of breaking bone.

But he had told me in a strangely dispassionate, almost detached way. He had assured me that he didn't think about it much and that he certainly didn't experience 'flashbacks' or nightmares about this nightmarish event. No, it wasn't this that he needed help with – it was the obsessional thoughts and anger about the trivial events that happened day after day.

'What did it feel like, lying on the road, watching him lifting the bar yet again?'

He closed his eyes.

'I knew I was going to die.'

'You were terrified.'

His covered his face with his hands, nodding slowly.

'And each time you see someone breaking the rules, it brings back the terror.'

'But . . . but these things don't make me frightened – they make me angry.'

Whenever Mark saw someone break the rules, his heart would race, his stomach churn, his skin become clammy and he would breathe faster. Unconsciously, his mind kept linking minor rule breaking to the murderous lawlessness which had nearly killed him; each time his body was engulfed by an adrenaline surge like the one he had felt on that awful night.

Yet Mark didn't put the label 'fear' on these adrenaline-induced symptoms of arousal. Instead, he interpreted the palpitations and sweats as signs of *anger*. But because there were so many of them, he was overwhelmed by such repeated surges of rage. And as they had no outlet or resolution, they could never be put to rest: this was why they became torturing, never-ending ruminations.

Mark gradually got better. Once he started to recognize the symptoms as fear rather than anger, he could do something about it: using simple cognitive behaviour therapy methods, I helped him to rationalize his fear, using his conscious mind to learn to create less alarming thoughts when he saw a rule being broken. He kept a diary of times when something happened which made him angry.

'Did you keep a record this week?'

'Yes,' he said, pulling out his notebook and handing it to me.

'You got very angry yesterday?'

'Yes, this guy on a train, with his earphones in his ears and this terrible buzzing, pounding music disturbing everyone sitting near him.'

'So what did you do?'

'I took a deep breath and closed my eyes, and tried to work out what the thoughts were that were making me so angry.'

'And . . .?'

'You know it sounds so stupid now . . . but you know what I realized I was thinking?'

'What?'

'That guy could beat someone to death,' he said with a wry half-smile.

'So what then?'

'I said to myself – don't be an idiot – he's just a selfish bastard who's going to be deaf by the time he's forty.'

'How did that make you feel?'

'A bit better . . . but I could still feel my heart pounding . . .'

'So what did you do?'

'I said to myself – you're scared, not angry . . . But there's nothing to be scared of. The guy's just stupid but harmless.'

'Did that change how you felt?'

'Yeah, a lot . . . but I had to do some of that breathing-relaxation stuff that you taught me – that worked.'

Mark's recovery didn't happen overnight – it takes a long time to unlearn emotional habits – but now that he wasn't chasing an emotional chimera with his unresolvable rage, Mark learned to put the right label on his adrenaline surges when they came upon him.

So where did that leave me in my search for resilience? What hadn't killed Mark, I realized, far from strengthening him, had very nearly finished him – only later did I find out quite how near to suicide he had been.

What Mark *had* taught me, however, with the help of Schachter and Singer's research, was that people facing adversity have to understand their emotions if they are to be resilient in the face of these bad times. That doesn't necessarily mean digging deep into early experiences, as may sometimes be necessary in psychotherapy – rather, it is about recognizing and then renaming the adrenaline surges that underlie all intense emotions, in a way that makes them more controllable.

So, resilient people can sometimes control bad feelings by thinking about them differently. But is there anything more positive that the swinging bridge phenomenon can say about Nietzsche?

When he said 'The day I'm not nervous is the day I quit', the American golfer Tiger Woods was turning anxiety on its head, changing it from, well . . . anxiety, to . . . what? – a sort of adrenaline rush for his game? When I read this quote, I saw that this was like what Mark had had to do, too – rethink an ambiguous emotional state into a less toxic one. But Tiger Woods seemed to be going further – he was turning the toxic into a positive tonic.

This is quite an achievement, because anxiety can really mess you up. Apart from winding your peripheral nervous system up in an unpleasant way, it makes everything seem worryingly uncertain and sabotages your feeling of being in control; this in turn saps your confidence, which actually makes you perform badly. It also clouds your mind and weakens your memory, both of which undermine your self-confidence and ability even more.

These are all signs of the brain's fear-primed avoidance system restraining its forward-looking approach system, as we saw in the last chapter. This in turn leads to the classic vicious cycle of anxiety that Gloria and Mark both endured.

But is there any way of not just breaking the vicious cycle but turning it into a virtuous one? Is there any science to back up Tiger Woods' belief that stressed people can turn anxiety on its head and use it to their advantage? Indeed there is, I discovered.

I had found out that we don't always read our own emotions accurately, as the swinging bridge study had shown. Even if you ask people to rate the attractiveness of people of the opposite sex after they've been to the gym, on average they think they're more attractive compared to when they haven't had exercise.[7] The brain's crude logic runs something like this: 'Ooh, my pulse is running high and my face is slightly flushed, so I must really like him/her.' But you can be tricked the other way, too, into regarding negative things as even more unpleasant: 'Ooh, my pulse is racing, so I really don't like him/her.'

So while anxiety is not a pleasant feeling, it shares many of the same characteristics as emotions like sexual arousal and anger. I had studied Schachter and Singer's then ten-year-old, but still startling, findings as an undergraduate at Glasgow University in

1972, but it wasn't until more than four decades later, in 2014, that I saw the logical therapeutic outcome of their discovery. This research showed how it's possible to harness anxiety and turn it into that most positive and energizing of emotions, *excitement*.

Sceptics may draw breath because the 'treatment' in the study I am going to describe was so very simple – but it was published in one of the most respected experimental psychology publications, the *Journal of Experimental Psychology*.[8]

Alison Brooks of the University of Pennsylvania put volunteers into various nerve-racking situations including: singing karaoke in front of strangers; public speaking; doing 'IQ-test' arithmetic problems under time pressure. But before each activity – and this was the 'treatment' – they spoke out loud a single sentence to themselves. That sentence was *I feel anxious, I feel calm* or *I feel excited*. They all wore heart-rate monitors and, in order to make them aware of their bodily symptoms, how fast their hearts were beating was displayed prominently to them during the experiment.

The results of this 'treatment' were exactly in line with what Tiger Woods said: people who told themselves that they felt excited not only felt more self-confident but also *performed better*, objectively measured, at all the tasks – singing, public speaking, even arithmetic. The opposite was true for those who said 'I feel anxious'.

Saying 'I feel calm', on the other hand, had no effect at all, either on performance or self-confidence. I scratched my head: how could a single sentence influence performance and self-confidence so much? Of course, this research was looking at normal, everyday levels of anxiety, not the sort of crippling, paralysing anxiety that patients like Gloria suffered. But, even so, the results were strong and convincing.

I remembered struggling – my own therapeutic self-confidence taking a battering along the way – to help Gloria try to control her terrible anxiety attacks. I tried to teach her how to relax her body and calm down her pulsating peripheral nervous system by slow breathing and muscular relaxation. But it only really worked for a short time, in my office, and she never seemed to be able to apply it in any of the multiple stress situations in which she found herself every single day. Why?

While reading Brooks' paper, the answer jumped out at me: calmness is the *opposite* state to anxiety – slow versus fast pulse, relaxed versus tense muscles, still versus churning stomach, dry versus sweaty skin . . . and so on. What an enormous challenge for anyone – but particularly for people like Gloria – to wrench their emotional state from one polar opposite to the other.

Wouldn't it have been easier to switch between emotional states that weren't such a leap? Of course! *Excitement's* symptoms are almost identical to those of anxiety – higher pulse and heart rate, facial flushing, churning stomach, and so on. So it *should* be easier to change from anxiety to excitement than from anxiety to calmness, which is what I had been trying to encourage with Gloria.

The swinging bridge experiment told us that emotions change if you change their *context*. But if a person with a fear of public speaking is waiting drenched in nervous sweat beside the podium about to give a public speech, the context is fixed – she can't change it. Or can she? I realized that she *can*. The most important context for any emotion is *inside her head*. Her mind can *create its own context*.

And that, I suddenly understood, was what the people in Brooks' experiment were doing – by saying to themselves 'I am excited', they were conjuring a new mental context for themselves which, like the swinging bridge, changed one emotion – anxiety, into another – excitement.

I could understand how feeling excited rather than anxious would make you feel more self-confident, but why should that make you *perform* better at singing, speaking, arithmetic, or, in Tiger Woods' case, golf? Brooks and her team had found at least part of the answer.

If you are about to do something that makes you nervous – say, go for an interview for promotion at work, or speak out about a controversial topic at a public meeting – then there are two broad mindsets you can adopt, *threat* or *challenge*. A threat mindset focuses your mind on the possible downsides of the situation – making a fool of yourself, for example – while a challenge mindset turns your attention to the upsides – making your name, impressing others, or just doing a good job, for that matter.

Alison Brooks discovered that saying 'I am excited' made people adopt a challenge rather than a threat mindset: those who declared themselves excited were more likely to see even singing for an audience as an opportunity for success rather than failure. But that still didn't quite explain those volunteers' better performance – why should I solve more problems or sing better just because I see them as a challenge?

Of course – the answer is *approach and avoidance*. A challenge mindset expects *reward* while a threat mindset anticipates *punishment*. Suddenly I saw the connection between this excitement study and the brain's left-right brain tug-of-war I had seen symbolized in Rodin's *The Kiss*.

Challenge maps on to the approach system, and threat to the avoidance system. Saying 'I am excited' in the face of nervous arousal switches your brain into approach mode by creating a challenge or opportunity mindset. The approach mode then increases dopamine activity, which focuses your attention and sharpens you mentally; that biochemical boost in turn sharpens your performance in maths, singing, public speaking. . . or indeed golf.

Once you are in approach mode, this not only makes you a little less anxious because of its tranquillizer-like properties, it also makes you less inclined to retreat and avoid because approach restrains the avoidance system. Avoidance also takes up precious mental space with worries about past, present and future threats. Simply saying 'I am excited', then, creates a double whammy by both boosting approach-linked opportunity thinking and at the same time lessening avoidance-related threat thinking.

I cast my mind back to Gloria again. I so wish that I had understood all this when I was treating her all those years ago. She was such an ambitious, talented person and maybe, just maybe, she could have learned to do what Tiger Woods does. I recalled so clearly the panic rising in her pale, drawn features at the mere thought of giving a job talk. 'I can't do it,' she'd sob between rapid, nearly choking breaths.

I encouraged her to try to do her relaxation routine, eyes closed, slowed breathing, relaxing her body bit by bit. I'm sure she would have tried very hard, sometimes even managing to reach a sort of calm. But there was always a part of her that was whip-tense, ready for new threat. And the moment her mind wandered, the prospect of the job interview or whatever the next threat in her life was would release again the full flood of anxiety.

Maybe Gloria could have felt more in control of these panics if she had learned to interpret them as signs of energy-giving excitement, as Tiger Woods does. She knew she was smart and that her work was of a high quality, and in her better moments she would have loved to show off her smartness to an inter-view panel. So there would have been something to work with, an ambition that maybe could have helped harness her nervous arousal into delivering a good performance. That might have been easier for her than trying to reduce her anxiety to a state of calmness which she seldom felt, except when on her own.

So, where was I? Like Mark whose bones were broken by a crim-inal with an iron bar, you may sometimes wake up in the early morning with a racing heart, gasping for breath and soaked in sweat. You may find yourself in the middle of the day with a knotted stomach and damp forehead, reliving whatever trauma has been.

But deep within every threat, every tragedy, lies a challenge. At the very least, it may be a matter of simply 'going on', in Beckett's terms: in very bad situations, the grim satisfaction of just putting one foot in front of the other, of getting through the next hour, the next day, with some dignity and grit may be the best that can be found.

But I felt that I had made some progress in understanding psychological strength, something to add to Beckett's 'going on'. Harnessing the adrenaline of fear and upset was at the centre of it: that is, finding a way to harness that arousal as fuel for chal-lenge rather than as a toxic, disabling threat.

Excitement wasn't a bad way of doing this and I was pretty sure that it would work well in much of life, whether in golf competitions or public speaking. Many of my patients hadn't suffered major traumas, and their anxiety was disproportion-ate to the setbacks they had encountered. For them, learning to rename their anxiety as excitement was a no-brainer – as indeed it has been for myself in everyday stresses that I, like everyone else, have had.

But Nietzsche wasn't talking about public-speaking anxiety. He was talking about events that literally nearly killed: accident, illness, injury, disability – but also death or injury to someone close to you that is the equivalent psychologically to a near-death experience. Saying 'Just re-label these nervous feelings as excitement' to someone who has just suffered a traumatic loss risks sounding both trite and off the mark.

Maybe 'excitement' isn't the right word for what's needed in these situations. How can someone feel excited after a loss? Perhaps he might be able to use some of the raw anxiety as an energy-giving spur to meet the challenge of simply going on. That was a small advance on simply 'going on', I thought – but still I felt I hadn't got to the heart of what makes some people grow in response to very tough times. Something was lacking.

I needed to regroup because I felt I had hit a dead end of sorts. What was missing?

Burning It All Clean?

What was missing was something that can energize people facing adversity in the way that excitement can. I needed to find a 'fuel' for Beckett's 'going on' that wasn't necessarily pleasant, but which nevertheless could help drive people forward to *go on* through adversity. Anxiety and fear may share adrenaline-arousal symptoms with sex and excitement, but tough times often put these positive emotions in short supply.

I was feeling a bit stuck, to be honest. My own personality does have a strong Pollyanna side to it, a tendency to see the silver lining in every cloud, which I suppose is why I have been so fascinated by stories of people who have been strengthened by adversity. But I know that I can irritate some people with this, particularly when my own life has been so relatively adversity-free. Life, for some, can be very tough, and asking them simply to flip a mental switch from one emotion to another, as if they were carefree students on a swinging bridge, can infuriate them, and rightly so.

I had to go back to the science to try to find an answer, but where to start amidst hundreds of thousands of academic papers? I decided to take two routes. First, I had to start with people who had suffered real trauma; for instance, who had for an awful moment thought they were going to die, and as a result developed post-traumatic stress disorder (PTSD). And, secondly, I wanted to look again at the positive and negative emotions of the approach and avoidance systems that I discussed in Chapter 3.

It was the awful shuddering, grinding pulsation of the falling helicopter that filled his mind, day and night, for months and years after the accident. And the noise – that tearing, ear-splitting crash of the rotors slicing through the cockpit and his crewmates' bodies. These feelings, sounds and images ran like a terrible multi-sensory movie in a ghastly, ever-repeating loop in his mind. Not for days, or months, but for years he had sat hunched in his chair in this hospital, a young, fit man whose mind had been taken over by an endlessly relived terror.

I have never seen a case of post-traumatic stress disorder as severe as this, before or since. The unending terror on the young oil worker's face stayed with me and, because I had worked with relatively few people suffering from PTSD, it focused my mind on fear as the cardinal emotion of trauma.

There are, of course, other symptoms of PTSD: for instance, images of the trauma intruding unbidden into the mind, causing

surges of adrenaline and fear, sometimes in waking life, sometimes as nightmares.

People try to avoid reminders of trauma, also. I remember in
1981 assessing a van driver in Scotland who had been parked
by the side of the road when a small car, a Hillman Imp, which,
unusually, was designed with its petrol tank at the front and
engine at the back, crashed into his van right in front of his eyes.
Frozen with shock in his cab, the doors jammed shut by the
impact, he watched helplessly as the petrol tank exploded and
the driver burned to death before his eyes.

The van driver went on to develop a phobia of Hillman Imps
and, whenever he saw one, he would suffer intense, terrifying
flashbacks to the accident. Worse, he began to feel anxious even
at the mere prospect of seeing one and so found it more and
more difficult to go out on the road. In the end he had to give up
his job. He became depressed and that is when he was referred to
me. Fortunately, I did manage to help him overcome his phobia
and eventually to get back to driving, but it was a long and
painful road for him.

The van driver's avoidance – physical or mental – is the second
typical symptom of traumatic stress. The effects can spread to
create a nest of complicated emotions ranging from guilt to
depression. Some become emotionally flat and unable to enjoy
things, even if they aren't fully depressed. They can also end up
feeling estranged from even those closest to them.

A famous example of this is Roméo Dallaire, who in 1993 was
appointed as Major General to the United Nations Assistance
Mission for Rwanda. The Canadian officer witnessed the geno-
cidal massacres of 1994 and he came back from Rwanda a
changed man. He suffered an extended mental collapse which
included four suicide attempts: 'there was an inability to commu-
nicate, an inability to speak to the family and talk about what

was happening to me,' he said in an interview with Canadian Television News in 2011.[9] 'There was no way to laugh any more, to love, to care and there was a sense of guilt in having survived when others had been killed.'

A fourth consequence of traumatic stress is arousal. Extreme stress can act like a supercharged bend in the road, driving the brain into a hyper-alert state via high levels of noradrenaline. This can tip people well beyond their Yerkes–Dodson peak and into a realm in which even the smallest sound can make them jump, when they can't sleep properly and can't concentrate because their minds are on constant, hyper-vigilant alert for new threats.

But there is another emotion that often haunts the person with PTSD. In a letter read out on Canadian radio in 2000, Roméo Dallaire wrote: 'the anger, the rage, the hurt and the cold loneliness that separates you from your family, friends and society's normal daily routine are so powerful that the option of destroying yourself is both real and attractive.'[10]

Anger had been a feature of the stress response of some people I had seen – Mark, for instance, the security guard who had been badly beaten. But only around 2000, when I had moved to Dublin, did I revisit Jeffrey Gray's approach and avoidance systems and begin to think about stress in terms of the balance between them.

The rough and ready notion that, broadly speaking, the left side of the brain was more approach-oriented and the right more avoidance-oriented, had wide currency by this time. The parallel for emotions was that positive ones like happiness were more left-lateralized in the brain, and negative emotions like fear, more right-lateralized.

But what about anger? Wasn't this a negative emotion? As researchers began to look at anger from the emotion approach-avoidance point of view, however, their perhaps too-neat left-positive/right-negative idea became problematic. Anger stood out as an anomaly in the approach-avoidance story. If it is a negative emotion, then it should be right-lateralized, like fear and anxiety. But several studies in the early noughties began to show that anger actually was more *left*-lateralized.[11]

Something had to change. Either anger had to be reconsidered as a positive emotion, or else we had to rethink the left-positive/right-negative idea.

What doesn't kill me often leaves some other scar, mental or physical, on people. It may also leave them feeling thwarted, stopped from doing what they once did. After an illness, accident or attack, emotional resilience doesn't come easy when it means having to deal with new limitations in your life such as disability, pain, stress, depression, loss of a loved one, financial ruin and so on. Restrictions make you frustrated, and frustration, I had learned in my first month of studying psychology at Glasgow University in 1970, often causes aggression – in other words, anger.

Then it clicked – left versus right brain activity had been mistakenly linked to positive and negative emotions, when in fact, its origins were in Jeffrey Gray's ideas about approach and avoidance. Anger may not be a pleasant emotion, but it is overwhelmingly an emotion that pushes you forward rather than pulling you back, and so is a classic emotion of *approach*. And so if I could rethink anger as an *approach* emotion, then I had both sorted out the apparent contradiction in the approach-avoidance findings and, perhaps more importantly, I had discovered something even more vital – a potential new fuel for *going on*.

Anger, then, is part of the left-hemisphere-linked approach system.[12] But can it act as that energizing emotion I had been looking for that, in the long run, can help strengthen us after bad things happen? No sooner was I feeling buoyed by thinking I had found another possible source of resilience than I saw that there was a problem, and it was a big one.

Anger is a very, very common feature in the emotional life of people with post-traumatic stress disorder.[13] It was, for instance, the overwhelming feeling in my patient Mark. But here's the problem: in a review of thousands of people like Mark, those with the *most* anger had the *worst* symptoms of PTSD.[14] Far from acting as an energizing *going-on* agent, anger had quite the *opposite* effect.

Maybe anger can be used as a short-term fuel to propel people beyond their traumatic symptoms in the longer term? In fact, the opposite seems true: the linkage between anger and traumatic symptoms appears to *strengthen* over time, over years and even decades.[15]

I was stuck again. I might have given up on this particular quest had I not come across, quite by chance, a quote attributed to the American author and poet Maya Angelou: 'Bitterness is like cancer. It eats upon the host. But anger is like fire. It burns it all clean.' Could it be that there are different types of anger, of which some are 'cleansing' and resilience-building while others 'eat upon the host'?

I spent some time studying the PTSD research. Yes, it seemed that there might indeed be two types of anger, which are usually referred to as 'anger-in' and 'anger-out'. People who show 'anger-out' tend to score highly on questions such as 'I am sarcastic to others', 'I say nasty things' or 'I am inclined to lose my temper'. 'Anger-in' individuals, on the other hand, tend to say things like 'I harbour grudges', 'I can be sullen' or 'I keep things in'.

Bottling up anger – anger-in, in other words – prolongs the symptoms of post-traumatic stress in a way that expressing your anger in an anger-out way does not.[16] Not that shouting and slamming doors reduce PTSD symptoms – by no means – it's just that they don't seem to be nearly as strongly involved in the prolonging of the trauma as bottled-up anger.

So, I wasn't really out of the woods. Yes, anger is an energizer, but bottled-up anger seems to make you more distressed rather than helping produce the Nietzschean resilience I was looking for. Even acted-out anger doesn't seem to help survivors 'go on'. So is Maya Angelou's aphorism just that – a baseless aphorism?

I returned to thinking about Mark. It was clear that in his case anger held him back rather than made him stronger. Mostly, his was 'anger-in' – bottled-up hostility towards boys on bikes and girls on buses who were completely oblivious to how angry they were making a stranger feel. Mark confused the symptoms of fear and anger in his mind so that even a minor surge of one emotion could set off the other, leading to a relentless cycle of anxious arousal fuelling fruitless rumination. Thinking about it, I could really understand why anger is such a pernicious partner of traumatic stress.

How could Mark's anger 'burn it all clean', when there wasn't anything to burn except his own tormented memories? Slamming doors and losing his temper with his wife may at least have let Mark vent some anger, but after a year or two it drove her away and then even that dysfunctional outlet for his anger was closed to him.

I had begun this search for an energizer that would help people to *go on*, and had thought I'd found it in anger. Yet my research on traumatic stress, and my experience with Mark and others, hadn't uncovered any such positive effects of anger. But before I abandoned the search I decided to take one last look at the emotion research literature to see if I could find any evidence at all that Maya Angelou was right – and, almost at once, I stumbled on something.

If I am insulted, it makes me angry, and anger switches on the left frontal lobe as part of the brain's approach system. So, my angry response to insult should energize me into approach, to *go on*. Except that sometimes it doesn't, and whether it does or not seems to depend on the *kind* of anger.

If I respond to the insult with some sort of action – for instance, answering back – then indeed my approach system switches on, with the left front part of my brain more active than the right.[17] But if I don't take action, and instead brood over the insult, then the rumination will make me uneasy and my anger will become tinged with anxiety. This is because I have unfinished business in my mind, in which a disturbing tension exists between wanting to respond, on the one hand, and stopping myself from doing so, on the other. Mental conflicts like this send unsettling jolts through my brain which feel like anxiety, hence the uneasy mix of nervous anger which begins to fill my ruminations.

Mark, I now realized, was exhausted and despairing because every time he saw someone break a rule he would do nothing and say nothing to the 'criminal'. Instead, it became just one more incident to ruminate over anxiously and angrily, day after day, night after night. Mark's anger, then, clearly did *not* energize his approach system. On the contrary, his sort of 'anger-in' fed his anxiety-fostering *avoidance* system.[18]

So anger as a response to 'What doesn't kill me' is worse than useless if you bottle it up and ruminate. For anger to be cleansing, it has to be expressed in action, but not aimless deeds like slamming doors or random temper outbursts. So, what sort of anger *does* cleanse and energize you positively?

I found another clue after more delving into research on emotion: it turns out that people choose anger as an emotion when they have to confront other people, but not when they are in non-confrontational situations like playing a game where co-operation, not competition, is required. What's more, in confrontational situations, anger makes people perform better, which is not the case in non-confrontational situations.[19]

Ah, I realized suddenly, anger is a *tool*. But anger only makes sense in our transactions with *other people* when it can help us get what we want – less shoddy service from a lazy car mechanic, for instance. Lonely anger against nameless people or abstract fate makes absolutely no sense and will most likely tip us into anxious avoidance rather than energized approach.

There are six basic emotions that play out across every culture and race. These are: fear, surprise, happiness, sadness, disgust and anger. Each emotion has played a different part in our evolutionary survival. Fear makes us alert and ready to run – its purpose is to avoid danger. Surprise alerts us to the unexpected and, because a predictable world is generally a safer world, it spurs us to work out what has happened and so regain some sense of predictability, and hence control, over the world.

Happiness is the consequence of our needs being met – or exceeded – and our goals fulfilled. It is a sign to keep doing whatever you're doing and that you are unlikely to die of hunger, loneliness or poverty. Sadness, on the other hand, is a response to loss and your bowed head and downcast eyes are physical signs that you have, for the time being, withdrawn from the fight. This may be an evolutionary signal that you are looking to be nurtured by the powerful and not to compete with them; sadness may elicit protective – and hence survival-offering – actions from your tribe. If you are lucky, that is. And disgust's purpose is to reduce your risk of being poisoned or infected by disease. It helps keep you away from deadly bacteria-rich bodily excreta, spoiled food and poisonous plants.

So, what about anger? Anger's role is at least partly to get you what you want or need when your goal is thwarted. It is very likely a *social* emotion whose purpose is to boost your chances of making someone else do what you want them to do so you can achieve your own goal. In other words, anger gives you a stronger hand in the game of life, with your anger increasing the chances of getting your way.[20] Angry negotiators get better deals on average than do non-angry negotiators (though not necessarily if they are dealing with people more powerful than themselves).[21]

The dog with the scariest, deepest growl whose teeth are bared the most is the one which is most likely to see its opponent back down, so saving them both the pain and injury which would follow a real fight. The angry human being is sending out similar signals, with the signs of anger – flushed face, clenched hands, rapid breathing – being like a fierce growl warning the other person of big future costs to them if they persist in blocking him by whatever it is they are doing or not doing.

If a massive rock falls and blocks the road and stops you from getting home, there is absolutely no point in getting angry with the rock or with the road – anger in these circumstances is totally useless. If, however, a fellow car driver has blocked the road through a piece of selfish parking, then anger indeed has a potentially useful purpose, assuming, of course, that the driver has not responded to your polite request to move: your anger is a signal of potential costs to him if he continues to block your goal. He doesn't know for certain what the costs are or whether there are any, but just appearing angry will have improved your negotiating position with him in this transaction.

Of course, a big man whose car is blocking the road may decide that the small man who is complaining about it does not threaten major physical costs to him. He may, however, also decide that this small, angry person is more likely to call the police than would the equivalent small, non-angry person. None of these millisecond calculations are entirely conscious, nor are they entirely predictable, but neither is poker predictable, and life has many similarities to a poker game.

So getting angry only makes sense in relation to specific other people who are blocking you in some way. It makes no sense whatsoever to be angry with the abstract – *people like that make me so angry* – because you're not playing poker with 'people like that' and you have no negotiating position to strengthen with them. The problem is, many people *do* torture themselves with useless anger against the abstract, as a patient of mine called Harry demonstrated all too clearly.

Harry was a handsome man of twenty-nine – tall, raven-haired and immensely attractive to his numerous girlfriends. He was endearingly narcissistic, with some cause, because, on top of his fashion-model looks, he was a clever and successful London businessman. But suddenly multiple sclerosis hit him like a truck and now he could only walk leaning heavily on an elegantly lacquered stick. It was an aggressive form of the disease and his girlfriends were falling away as fast as they had been drawn to him a mere two years earlier.

It was a brutal blow to a young man in his prime, and who could expect any response from him other than emotional turmoil? But that turmoil was amplified and prolonged by a burning anger that tortured him, day after day and night after sleepless night. Harry's anger was not directed against a particular person, however – rather, it was anger against the breaching of an *abstract principle*.

Belief in this principle – and the anger triggered by its being breached – has prolonged the suffering of countless millions of people. Why? Because the principle is a myth – and a cruel one, at that. Harry would blurt out his complaint again and again, often tearfully, his handsome face blotched with anger: 'It's not *fair!*' Harry, who considered that he had lived a good life, believed he had had a great injustice inflicted on him by being stricken with multiple sclerosis. And it made him feel very, very angry.

On 23 May 2014, a young man uploaded a video to YouTube. He gave a long, angry monologue to camera, including these words: 'I'm twenty-two years old and I'm still a virgin. I've never even kissed a girl. I've been through college for two and a half years, more than that actually, and I'm still a virgin. It has been very torturous. College is the time when everyone experiences those things such as sex and fun and pleasure. Within those years, I've had to rot in loneliness. *It's not fair* [my italics].'[22]

Elliot Rodger completed his upload, stabbed his three student flatmates to death and drove off to shoot dead three more people and injure thirteen others before killing himself.[23] The title he gave his final video was 'Elliot Rodger's Retribution', indicating that this young man did what he did at least in part as revenge against what he saw as the unfairness of a world in which young women were attracted to other men but not to him.

Of course, Rodger had many different problems and he didn't kill six people simply because he believed an injustice had been done to him. Nevertheless, it is reasonable to assume that his stated belief that *it's not fair* partly fuelled the anger that drove him to mass murder.

Harry's anger hurt no one but himself. But, like Elliot Rodger, he was tormented by an anger against injustice, against the feeling that he had been 'done the dirty on' by some abstract breaching of the principle of fairness in the world. But this anger had no target because there was no judge who could be swayed by Harry's rage.

I would define Harry's as a classic case of 'anger-in', which contributes to an internal stew of adrenaline-fuelled arousal whose diffuse symptoms sparked off anxiety on top of the anger. This angry-anxious cycle of ruminations would have activated his brain's right-sided avoidance system, as recent research confirms[24] and this, as we saw in Chapter 3, would have led to the inhibition of his approach system. But it was an energetic, goal-focused approach that this young man so badly needed to square up to the challenges of his disease and disability. Instead, his mental energies were squandered in a fruitless rage against a myth. Because, of course, there is no basis for believing that the natural world is fair and that the virtuous will be rewarded by an illness-free life.

So where was I in my search for a redeeming, energizing anger that might fuel a Nietzschean will to go on? Not very far, I had to admit to myself – until, that is, a very annoying study caught my eye.

The annoyance that the volunteers in this research had to endure was considerable. Here is how the researchers described what they did to their volunteers:

The stress-challenge tasks included: 1) counting backward by 7s from 9095; 2) mentally calculating arithmetic problems taken from the Wechsler Intelligence Test; and 3) counting backward by 13s from 6233 . . . To accentuate the socially stressful nature of the tasks, participants were informed of each error they made and urged to go faster by a harassing experimenter. Participants were also told that these tasks were diagnostic of general intelligence and that their responses would be compared with other participants' scores. Thus, the tasks and the experimenter could be justifiably seen as annoying.[25]

Funnily enough, not everyone was 'annoyed' by this task. Analysis of their recorded facial expressions showed that some people actually displayed signs of anxiety and, not surprisingly, their blood pressure increased along with levels of the stress hormone cortisol circulating around their bodies. Were the angry people even more stressed, I wondered, in the light of all the findings about the negative effects of anger I had been finding?

No, was the surprising finding. In their bodily responses, the angry group showed much less stress. How could this be, I mused – was this annoyance not a symptom of classic 'anger-in'? Perhaps not, because they were showing their anger through their facial expressions in a situation in which the people who were making them angry – the researchers – were actually *there*. In this situation, anger served the purpose of a sort of threat signal, hopefully warning off the researchers from inflicting any more annoying activities and so was really 'anger-out'.

And then it came to me: could it be that for anger to have some resilience-building benefits it must have a *purpose*? Showing anger to someone who is harassing you does have a purpose, even if it doesn't work. But feeling angry afterwards, cursing them in your mind, perhaps, has no function because that person is no longer there. Anger is an instrument in our relationships with other people. But, more importantly, anger is an emotion with a goal – to remove the blockage or threat that has roused it.

Deprived of a goal, anger is like a car engine disconnected from its wheels – its revving becomes a useless whine which makes the car rattle and shudder but go nowhere. In striving for some grip, this inward-directed energy revs faster and faster because there is no resistance from the road – just like angry ruminations that blend with anxiety to torment with their very fruitlessness. Anger will only 'burn it all clean' if the engine is connected to its wheels.

Maybe I was beginning to get a grip on anger, I thought. But then I stumbled upon a quote from Aristotle which took me aback – he had got there a couple of thousand years before me: 'Anybody can become angry – that is easy, but to be angry with the right person and to the right degree and at the right time and for the right purpose, and in the right way – that is not within everybody's power and is not easy.'[26]

Anger has to have a purpose and if it doesn't it will undermine me in facing *what doesn't kill me*, and won't energize me into squaring up to the challenge. Or, as Mark Twain put it: 'Anger is an acid that can do more harm to the vessel in which it is stored than to anything on which it is poured.'

So I had come a long way in my quest for this 'fuel' which could energize people into *going on* after bad things have happened. When excitement and optimism are in short supply as sources of 'approach', anger can be that fuel – it may even be able to *burn clean* – but it is like a loaded gun which, if not handled properly, is more likely to wound the owner than her enemy.

Some of us can cultivate an angry approach to life, particularly if it has dealt us some bad hands. This can make some people chronically hostile, inclined to dislike and mistrust other people and interpret other people's behaviour as selfish and threatening. People like this are walking cauldrons of angry rumination – Mark had become like this after his experiences – and this is bad for their health, raising their blood pressure, cortisol and stress levels to the point that they are more at risk from heart and other diseases.[27]

I had helped Mark get over his problems by encouraging him to reinterpret ordinary events as non-threatening, and by recognizing that there was trauma-related anxiety mixed up with his anger. But researchers had in the meantime developed new ways of helping chronically angry people express their anger in constructive ways of the sort that Aristotle recommends.[28]

Constructive anger uses its *approach energy* to spell out clearly and in a controlled way precisely why you are angry with someone and what you expect them to do about it. For example: 'You have needlessly kept me waiting for the last twenty minutes while you chatted on the phone – I want you to serve me immediately.' Your anger is visible to them in your expression and voice, but your words are clear and factual rather than inflated and emotional. If you train chronically hostile people to express their anger constructively, it turns out, you can bring down their blood pressure and help them be less tormented by angry ruminations.[29]

This sort of training might have helped Mark, too. He could, for instance, have suggested to the girl on the bus that she might give her seat to the old man. One reason he didn't was that he was worried that he might lose control and start shouting. He had never learned to express anger in a controlled, constructive way and his bitter experience was that when he did give vent to his anger, say, in temper outbursts, it generally did him no good, leaving him feeling exposed, anxious and ashamed because he had lost control. But, worst of all, these outbursts had driven his wife away. No wonder he kept his anger locked inside.

Anger, however, is not like a dam behind which pressure inexorably rises as it fills up, leading to catastrophe unless it is released. Angry Mark stopped being so angry once he started to interpret his angry feelings as symptoms of anxiety. Emotion arises, in part at least, out of how we *think* about the situation we are responding to. Say I am waiting to buy a ticket in a crowded station and I feel someone elbowing me from behind. I turn round, angry at such rude impatience, to find that I have been elbowed by a blind woman, disoriented by the crowd, who is trying to find her way through. My anger is deflated immediately like a punctured balloon by my sudden reinterpretation of the situation.

I had a friend whose father, who had major, long-standing psychiatric problems, committed suicide. My friend was understandably very distressed and this continued for many months. Only after a while did I realize that his upset was composed as much of anger as of grief. I sat down to talk to him about it and he railed against his father's selfishness and cruelty in killing himself. He really was tormented by these angry feelings, not sleeping properly and also feeling increasingly anxious. So I asked him, 'If your father had died of cancer, would you feel like this?' He replied, no, of course not. I said, 'Your father was a sick man' – he had had severe psychotic episodes over the years – 'and his suicide was a symptom of his illness, so why are you so angry with him?'

The change was remarkable and immediate. My friend's altered perspective on his father's death stopped him being angry and, because this sort of fruitless anger – his poor, dead father was now tragically immune from it – had inevitably become a blood-pressure and cortisol-raising 'anger-in', his stress levels plummeted, too. His wife told me later that she had found it incredible how quickly the clouds had lifted from him and that his anger against his father never returned.

But, of course, not all anger can be reinterpreted away as easily as this. Though Mark responded well to the cognitive behaviour therapy, he continued to experience brief relapses from time to time, periods when the rage he felt against the man who had tried to kill him swept through him like a poison. But these became less and less common as he became better at reinterpreting the things that happened. For instance, he began to realize that this hadn't been an attack on him as an individual; this was a bad criminal doing his job as a bad criminal, and anyone blocking his way would have suffered the same fate as Mark. It wasn't specifically Mark he had tried to kill: his target was just a man in a uniform. Depersonalizing it in this way took some of the sting out of the anger for Mark, making him feel less generally victimized as an individual, and took down his stress levels another few notches.

Mark had to do a lot of this sort of mental reworking over the months that I was seeing him. The jargon word for what he was doing is 'reappraisal' and it can be a powerful tool in mastering strong emotions which may otherwise gain the upper hand. All the frontal lobes of the brain are involved in this mentally demanding work – left and right sides, inside and outside surfaces all working together – reworking the patient's perspective on bad emotional reactions to tough events. When the frontal lobes work together like this, they send signals to the emotion centres of the brain – a region called the amygdala, in particular – and reduce emotion-generating activity there.[30]

Rethinking distress in this sort of way works like a side-effect-free tranquillizer, directly diminishing unpleasant feelings of fear and anger by lowering the activity in the brain regions that produce them. But it takes hard work and a lot of thinking, which can be very difficult for many people, particularly when their thoughts are clouded by the very stress they are trying to cope with.

Mark hadn't been able to do any 'reappraisal' before I saw him, although he *was* trying to cope with the emotional turmoil, particularly in the months before his wife finally left him. However, he was employing a method which people use an awful lot, but which, as research published around the millennium has shown, is pretty ineffective. The method Mark used was to try to bottle up his feelings of anxiety and anger, and try to *suppress* the thoughts that went with them.

In one of the studies showing this, volunteers watched gruesome videos of things like animal slaughter and human surgery. Some were asked to do what Mark had tried to do, namely suppress their emotional responses by deliberately not turning away and not registering disgust in their expression, for example – these were the *suppressers*. Others were asked to adopt the stance of a professional while watching them; by focusing on the technique of the surgeons, for instance, as if they were going to be asked to carry out the procedure in future – these were the *reappraisers*.[31]

Both groups reported that they felt less emotion when compared to a control group who just watched the films, but there the similarities ended. Around four to five seconds after the video began, the reappraisal group's frontal lobes showed a surge of activity and the brakes were applied to key emotion centres, including in a region called the insula and also to the amygdala. In the suppress group, on the other hand, activity in the insula and amygdala *increased*.

Suppressing emotions without reappraising them, as Mark had tried to do for years before his life fell apart with his wife's departure, increases adrenaline-linked arousal responses including raised heart rate, blood pressure and skin sweatiness. It also makes your memory poorer,[32] probably because suppressing an emotion requires fairly constant activity of the frontal lobes. Reappraising, on the other hand, though hard work at first, doesn't make the same sort of constant demands on the frontal lobes as suppression does.

Suppression has other costs, too. Because inhibition is rather a blunt instrument, and because emotions like fear, sexual arousal and anger have so many overlapping arousal 'symptoms', suppressing a negative emotion almost inevitably leads to the suppression of other positive emotions, too. People whose style it is to suppress emotions rather than reappraise them don't share their emotions, whether positive or negative, with other people nearly as much as reappraisers do, and as a result are on average less well liked by other people.[33] This is because we tend to trust and like people who are open and self-disclosing.

Nietzsche and the Swinging Bridge

Nietzsche, a great believer in man's existential 'will to power', would probably have approved of the possibility of our mastering our emotions through an act of conscious reinterpretation of the circumstances causing these feelings. He may not have been interested much in fear changing into sexual arousal on a Canadian swinging bridge, but I'm pretty sure he would have been curious about how we can best harness and control anger in our 'will to power' over our destinies.

As we have learned in this chapter, however, anger is a tricky and complex emotion, which can be dangerous when it is turned inwards or suppressed rather than reinterpreted. But from all the research into reappraisal and from the very first classic study by Schachter and Singer into fear and excitement, it is clear that anger and excitement can sometimes be mentally re-engineered just as fear and sexual arousal can. Anger against anonymous others or against fate *has* to be reappraised. Justified anger against real people, on the other hand, can help you *approach* and so energize you in facing up to the challenge.

Such simple switches of mental set as we saw on the swinging bridge completely changed the whole psychology – indeed, physiology – of the people involved. Instead of provoking the inhibition and fear of their brains' right-half avoidance system, their changed mental set switched on the left-half approach system, with thoughts of sex overwhelming fear of death.

In the course of thinking about my past cases in the light of an enormous amount of new research which was not available at the time when I was seeing them, I had come to the conclusion that, as the founder of cognitive behaviour therapy Aaron Beck had long asserted, our mental set determines what we feel, think and do to a quite remarkable extent. By a simple mental flip, for instance, diffuse bodily sensations which feel like anxiety in one context can be transformed through reinterpreting them as excitement, into an energy-giving invigoration.

These findings also helped me edge towards a fuller understanding of emotional resilience. I will be made stronger to the extent that I reappraise, rather than suppress, my emotions. I can use anger, but only with great care and to a clear purpose.

I was making quite a bit of progress. What doesn't kill me can make me mentally stronger by offering me more control over my emotions through reappraisal and focused, targeted anger. But emotional strength is only one kind of strength. Can we be strengthened in other ways? Can, for instance, the stress of 'what doesn't kill me' also make me smarter? This is the question I set out to answer in the next chapter.

5

How Can Stress Make You Smarter?

The telephone rang one day in my Trinity College office. On the line was one of our former PhD students, now a post-doctoral Fellow working on the Irish Longitudinal Study on Ageing, just a few buildings away. This study of several thousand adults over fifty aims to find out how people age over time, and what makes some people age better than others. But I was surprised by the content of this call, because it was concerned with something about which I know very little – sexual abuse.

Joanne Feeney, the researcher, told me she had discovered that roughly one in fifteen of the fifty- to ninety-year-olds she was studying reported that they had been sexually abused as children. This wasn't the surprise – such figures are fairly typical of research studies worldwide. As is usually the case, in adulthood these abuse victims were more depressed and also less physically healthy than their contemporaries. This fairly typical finding is explained by the prolonged stress-linked damage to the body caused by being subjected to early abuse. So the picture here fitted with what we already knew.

Except that it didn't.

Joanne's research had unearthed a remarkable fact about the sexually abused people. Despite all their other health and emotional problems arising from this ghastly early trauma, they were cognitively better on objective tests of memory, thinking, problem-solving and attention, and were quicker mentally than non-abused people in the study of the same age, social and educational background.[1] Because of the size of the study – nearly 7,000 people – Joanne and her colleagues could rule out other physical, social and mental factors that might have caused the differences. But it was also a real puzzle. Did any other research back this up, Joanne wondered. Hence the phone call.

I could find only one other study which had addressed cognitive abilities in older people who had suffered childhood physical, mental or sexual abuse.[2] But, sure enough, those people were mentally sharper than a control group, though it wasn't possible to disentangle the separate effects of the different types of abuse. That being said, other, less severe, types of early stress such as losing a parent or being bullied at school had the opposite effect on mental sharpness, this study showed. So it was a complicated picture.

This study and Joanne's got me wondering. Did any other types of stress affect mental sharpness? I discovered some Dutch research that measured cognitive abilities in more than a thousand people in their early seventies, and then again three years later.[3] The seventies is a difficult decade for many, with new pressures on people such as a spouse succumbing to serious illness. Conflicts with families can also spring up during the major changes that are so common at this time of life. The Amsterdam group were no exception – over three-quarters of them reported having experienced at least one very significant 'life event' during the three years.

Sure enough, those whose partners had suffered a serious illness showed *better* cognitive function than those who had not. What's more, people who had run into severe conflict with other people – family, friends, neighbours, etc. – were *also* cognitively sharper three years later, something also found in another study in the USA.[4]

So, the early abuse-better cognitive function link wasn't a completely isolated one. But now came the hard bit – why? It so happened that Joanne's call had come at a time when I was in the middle of trying to solve a quite different problem. So I put her puzzle to the back of my mind and got back to my own quest. Funnily enough, in searching for the solution to my own problem I was to stumble on a possible answer to hers.

The Swedish Twins

Dementia is a lurking epidemic that, if we don't do something about it, will swamp our economies and our health services. It is becoming more common because we are living longer – the older you are the more likely you are to suffer from it, to the extent that almost half of ninety-five-year-olds have dementia.[5] In other words, the good news of increasing life expectancy is tempered by the bad news of a dramatic rise in dementia. In my view we need to be as concerned about this as about global warming.

The most common type of dementia is Alzheimer's disease, for which there is currently no effective treatment and whose causes are not well understood. The only way to be absolutely sure that someone has Alzheimer's is to study their brain after death. Doing that, you see a depressing picture of an organ shrunk by the death of millions of its neurons. The Alzheimer's brain is sprinkled with growths of a protein called amyloid, which poisons the neurons, and there are also tangles of another substance called tau, which cause havoc inside brain cells.

One thing we do know is that there is a genetic factor in Alzheimer's disease. A tragically early but mercifully relatively rare form of the illness that can strike people before they are sixty has a strong genetic element. But most cases happen later in life and get inexorably more common with age, as people's ageing brains become clogged up with those damnable proteins. Surely we have here a dreadful medical condition about which psychologists have nothing to say beyond cheering on their biologist colleagues in their desperate search for a molecular or biochemical answer to the problem?

Maybe – except for one very strange fact about Alzheimer's disease: the more education you have had in your life, the smaller your chance of showing symptoms of the disease. Hundreds of studies have shown this, one of which found that the risk of Alzheimer's in people with the lowest level of education was as much as *six times* greater as for those with the highest.[6]

I had been studying this strange fact about dementia since I came to Dublin in 1999 and this was what I had been mulling over when Joanne called me about the sexual abuse data. How could it be, I asked myself, that an apparently purely biological condition like Alzheimer's is so affected by something as *social* as schooling? How could teachers and books be such powerful antidotes to those poisonous proteins doing their dark work of killing off brain cells?

The fallacy of assuming that correlation means cause is one of the first lessons I learned when I started studying psychology. Yet every day I read in the media about scientific studies showing that people who do x are more likely to suffer from y and hence x causes y. Quite early in my career, I learned a good lesson about why you have to be sceptical about such studies.

In the early 1980s, when I was researching alcohol problems in Scotland, the editor of the *British Medical Journal* asked me to write an editorial for the *BMJ*. My brief was to examine recent research which suggested that even light social drinkers suffered loss of cognitive and memory function – a sobering fact for the majority of people in the Western world, myself included, who are social drinkers. So I looked carefully at the research and, indeed, several studies showed that the more drinks a person has per week the poorer their cognitive function[7] – even at very low levels of consumption. Indeed, one of the main advocates of the dangers of even light drinking on brain function wrote a book of anecdotal case studies of people whose lives had gone off the rails, ostensibly due to small amounts of alcohol disrupting their mental functioning. These cases studies purported to show how, when they gave up drinking, their lives came together and their problems were resolved. Very convincing.

But it was all wrong. This was because it was based on the fallacy that correlation equals cause. As I looked into the research, it dawned on me that there was a third factor which was linked to drinking and cognitive function. In this case it was IQ.[8]

It turns out that on average people with lower IQ levels tended to drink more and also performed more poorly on tests of memory, thinking and attention. As I looked more closely at the data I found that if you controlled for IQ using statistical methods, the link between social drinking and cognitive test performance completely disappeared. In other words, moderate drinking does not cause damage to the brain or cause cognitive problems.

In the sexual abuse study that began this chapter, Joanne was able to take into account levels of education and other factors that could have made them mistake correlation for cause. But, of course, their study was still based on correlations and they couldn't be 100 per cent certain that the sexual abuse was 'causing' the better cognitive performance of its victims: and even if we could be sure of such a causal link, the severe and lifelong health and emotional damage caused by the abuse overwhelmingly outweighed any of the cognitive effects we observed.

So was I falling into the familiar trap of confusing correlation with cause in trying to explain the strange connection between education and Alzheimer's disease? Perhaps there was a third variable that was creating a spurious linkage between them?

The most likely possible culprit was a common genetic profile that both raises IQ – and hence education level – and also reduces the brain's vulnerability to Alzheimer's. This 'good brain' theory assumes that educational level has no cause-and-effect relationship with Alzheimer's, but that there is a single genetic cause for both higher IQ and resistance to Alzheimer's.

I was rather stumped by this – until I came across a study of thirty-three pairs of identical Swedish twins.[9] In each of these pairs of twins – who, remember, were genetically identical – one had dementia and the other had not. The researchers looked at the level of education the demented twins had received versus the non-demented twins. Some had left school at the minimum legal age while others had stayed on in education. Among the non-demented twins, twelve had left school at the minimum age, while twenty-one had continued their education. And what about the demented twins? The vast majority of them – twenty-five in all – had left school as soon as it was legally possible, while only eight had stayed on.

So genetics couldn't explain the education–dementia link because the twins were genetically identical. Now I was more confident that there was something real going on here. Education, it seems, could reduce the risk of dementia. But why? And how? And how did this fit in with the strange link Joanne and her colleagues had discovered between sexual abuse and mental sharpness?

Learning as Neurosurgery

What *does* education do to the brain that strengthens it against dementia? That was the puzzle. Is education a sort of non-invasive neurosurgery injecting a mysterious something into the brain that protects it against disease? If so, it is far from a perfect operation. Tragically, many highly intelligent, highly educated people, such as Iris Murdoch, the celebrated Anglo-Irish novelist, succumb to Alzheimer's. But, however imperfect, what is the nature of this 'neurosurgery'?

I found a possible answer in a study of the brains of a class of German medical students studying for their final exams.[10] They agreed to have their brains scanned three times – three months before the exams, then just after they had spent three months studying, with a final scan three months after the end of the exams.

The researchers measured the thickness of the grey matter in different parts of their brains using magnetic resonance imaging (MRI). When they analysed the brain scans just after three months of gruelling study, they saw an effect that no neurosurgery in the world can yet achieve – their brains had *grown*.[11] To be specific, a part of their brains called the parietal cortex – billions of neurons in the grey matter towards the back and top of the brain – had expanded. Three relaxing months later, the students' gains in their parietal cortexes had been maintained, but there had been no more growth.

But something even more interesting had happened in another part of their brains. This is an area of the brain called the hippocampus. In a famous study, researchers at University College London had found that area had expanded in London taxi drivers.[12] Unlike taxi drivers in many cities, who are often incomers with a scanty knowledge of the locality, London taxi drivers have to pass something called 'The Knowledge', which entails memorizing the entire street map of London and all its possible routes and short cuts. If you go to London and see people riding around the streets on mopeds with clipboards attached to their handlebars, that is what they are doing. To become a London taxi driver as of 2015, you must spend two years learning, and then be tested on your 'Knowledge' of this enormous, sprawling metropolis, without the help of any satellite navigation system.

I find this particular piece of research so exciting because the hippocampus is the key structure which fails in Alzheimer's: it is the crucial part of the brain for laying down new memories, moment to moment, day to day and month to month. A person with the disease will usually have less of a problem remembering things that happened years ago, but will forget what was said or happened a few minutes before. This is because the hippocampus – the part of the brain that is ultrasensitive to the disease – is failing. So what had happened to the German medical students' brains? As was the case for the taxi drivers, the rear part of their hippocampus had grown. And there was one more, quite remarkable, finding: unlike their parietal cortexes, which stopped growing after the studying stopped, this region *kept on growing* for the three months after the exams ended.[13] Learning remodelled the brain more surely than any neurosurgeon could.

So what had the case of the Swedish twins taught me? Had the more educated twins so strengthened their brains through staying on at school that it had given them some protection against dementia? Was it possible that, even if the dreaded Alzheimer's insinuated its way into their brains, they kept on functioning for longer because they had bigger, better connected networks to fall back on?

Maybe the more educated Swedish twins with no obvious signs of dementia actually had as much of the rogue proteins, amyloid and tau, in their brains as the demented ones, but because education had enlarged and strengthened their brains – particularly their posterior hippocampi and parietal cortices, if we accept the medical student findings – then they could still keep remembering and thinking *despite* the disease's presence. Only when the disease was really advanced might it show up in day-to-day memory loss in the better educated twins: indeed, it might never show up because they die of old age before their boosted brains have lost the battle against the disease.

This effect of learning and education on dementia has been given the name 'cognitive reserve' and, when post-mortems have been carried out on people with high cognitive reserve, they really do have *thicker* layers of grey matter in the cortex and many more brain cells per cubic millimetre than those with less cognitive reserve.[14]

So that all makes sense . . . or does it? What gave me pause was a study I read of some Chicago citizens in their eighties. An initial measurement was taken of their memories and cognitive abilities and they were followed up until death, an average of three years later. Post-mortems were then carried out to see how much Alzheimer's and other dementia pathology there was in their brains. For some, the picture was pretty clear – the more tangles of Alzheimer's tau protein they had in their brains, the poorer their memory and cognitive ability as measured three years earlier. But, for others, there was no such relationship and more tau protein in their brains was *not* linked to poorer memory.

So what distinguished these two groups? Was there some elixir that allowed half of these eighty-year-olds to keep mentally sharp in spite of toxic proteins in their brains? Was it some protective chemical in their diet, or some drug that had been prescribed to them for another condition? No, it wasn't. Again the answer was a social one.

It was their friends and their family.

The crucial ingredient, it turned out, was contact with children, relatives and/or friends close enough that you could confide in them and call on them for help. The number of such people the eighty-year-olds saw at least once a month constituted the size of their social network. Those in the top 10 per cent of social network size showed no relationship between tau protein in their brains and their memory abilities.[15]

There was, however, one more ingredient in the recipe for 'cognitive reserve' and when I discovered it, somewhere in that corner of my mind that was still puzzling over the sexual abuse findings, a small bell rang. This extra ingredient that seemed to boost resistance to dementia was *mental activity*. Study after study found that older people who were mentally engaged doing things like reading and writing, or taking part in hobbies or games, stayed mentally sharper and were less at risk of Alzheimer's than those who were not.[16]

The old correlation vs cause trap raised its head – maybe people who were already in the very early stages of the disease simply weren't able to keep mentally engaged. So the only way I could be sure that mental activity was causing the mental sharpness rather than vice versa was if I could find a study in which people were randomly assigned to mental activity and then were compared with those who were not.

So I searched the scientific literature and found such a study. Researchers at the University of Berlin in Germany had randomly assigned healthy women aged seventy to ninety-three to a course on which they learned how to use computers over a six-month period. Compared to women who weren't mentally engaged in this way, at the end of the training they showed better memory and general mental sharpness.[17] A review by Sydney researcher Michael Valenzuela of all the randomized trials which had been carried out confirmed this conclusion.[18] So, I was persuaded; it isn't just the number of years of education you have when you are young which strengthens your cognitive reserve: continuing to use your brain into old age and having a rich social network also do this.

I was still no closer to understanding a possible link between very bad early experiences and later cognitive function, but I had made some progress in understanding cognitive reserve: the Swedish researchers had managed to rule out genetics as an explanation for the education–dementia link, suggesting that education is *causing* people to be somewhat protected against Alzheimer's disease. Then the German medical students show that that staple of modern education – studying for exams – does indeed physically grow the brain.

But other elements of cognitive reserve like a mentally stimulating job or a good social network *also* seem to bolster the brain against dementia. Was I to believe that they too expanded the brain in the way that studying for finals had in the medical students? I hadn't yet properly cracked the cognitive reserve–dementia link. Frustrated, I went back to the journals searching for more ideas.

Couch Potato Blight?

It was the television reference that caught my eye. Apparently, while keeping your mind active generally seemed to go together with greater mental sharpness, this does not apply to watching television.[19] Why might that be, I wondered, so I began to burrow into the television-watching research.

I discovered that watching television over longish periods tends to sap your mental energies, colloquially speaking. One review of the research concluded that watching television while relaxing was both cognitively undemanding and linked to feelings of passivity and drowsiness.[20] That made sense to me: after several hours slumped on a sofa watching TV, I am so relaxed I feel ready for embalming.

Young and middle-aged people often use TV to escape from the stressful demands that are being made on them, but older people don't tend to use it like that and the more they watch, the less happy they feel. And this, it turns out, isn't because they aren't doing other more enjoyable leisure activities: it is the amount of time spent watching TV, not the amount of time they spend on other leisure activities, which determines how satisfied and engaged with life they feel.[21]

I spent some time trying to remember what it feels like after a long evening in front of the TV. The phrase 'feelings of relaxation, passivity, and drowsiness' really captures the sluggishness of its effects. Something was glimmering at the back of my mind. That sluggishness is a bit like how you feel first thing in the morning – dull and slow, for a few minutes at least. And what is behind that feeling? Of course – *low arousal*. Could television watching's at best neutral and at worst negative effects on memory and thinking be because of its lowering of arousal in our brains? Does extended TV watching, in other words, have a sort of reverse 'bend-in-the-road' effect that pulls you back down below the low-arousal Yerkes–Dodson peak?

After seeing the results of these studies showing that TV watching reduced arousal, I was intrigued by the notion that the converse might be true: that mentally challenging activities and social networks repeatedly *boost* arousal and this is how they protect the brain from dementia. My own research that

I described in Chapter 1 had found that lifting low arousal to the top of its inverted U-curve improved 'executive control' in brain-injured people so that they were able to be mentally more on the ball. So, do cognitive reserve activities – hobbies, education and social networks, for instance – work in a similar way, by upping low arousal levels in otherwise understimulated people, to a Yerkes–Dodson tipping point of mental performance?

It was a slightly off-the-wall hypothesis and, in proposing it, I was setting myself a big task. My own research had shown that our performance can be ramped up by challenge – as we saw with John, the TV cameraman in Chapter 1 whose mental sharpness depended on challenge-triggered arousal. And that research also showed that the chemical messenger noradrenaline is a key ingredient of this energizing arousal.

I was still far from solving the puzzle with which I began this chapter, but then, in 2010, I found myself embarking on a quite different journey, trying to test the possibility that arousal and its noradrenaline partner might play a key role in protecting people against dementia. It was a journey that would take me two years to complete.

The Tipping Point's Big Test

My hypothesis was the following: mental challenge and social networks bring the brain to an optimal zone of arousal and it is this continued arousal that is protecting the brain from dementia. My motivation to test this hypothesis was given a boost when I discovered that four cognitive reserve ingredients – education, IQ, mentally demanding job and mental activity – taken together almost *halve* the risk of Alzheimer's disease.[22] No medical treatment, no drug, has a fraction of that efficacy. These are quite astonishingly large effects, but if I was to make any use of them I had to understand *how* they work.

I started by looking at some of the basic laboratory research on what is known as 'environmental enrichment'. Many hundreds of studies, I discovered, have shown that mice and rats which are kept in cages in which there is a variety of objects to explore show much better memory and cognitive abilities than those which have been kept in standard, relatively austere, environments.[23] What's more, they also grow extra brain cells![24]

I was, of course, in my own mind comparing this 'enrichment' of laboratory rodents with the cognitive enrichment that humans experience when they meet other people, play games, solve problems and learn new things. Could these be similar phenomena and, if so, is there a common mechanism underpinning their effects in animals and humans?

Though many hundreds of studies show the beneficial effects of environmental enrichment in small animals, I couldn't find any which attempted to answer the question, *how* does it happen? Until, that is, I read a brilliant French study that set my scientist's pulse beating faster.

What is it about enriched environments, the researchers at the University of Lyon asked, that improves memory and grows new brain cells? They knew that mice – for whom smell is the dominant sensory channel – that were kept in cages with a rich mix of smells both showed better memory and had new brain cells emerge in the key smell regions of their brains. But in addition the French researchers asked this very clever question: what would happen if you gave the mice a whole mix of many different smells every day for forty days, versus *giving them one new smell every day* over the same period.

If you put yourself into a mouse's skin for a moment, you will appreciate a paradise of scents – pepper, star anise, fennel, cinnamon, garlic, onion, ginger, juniper berries, clove, nutmeg, lemon, celery, cumin, chocolate, cardamom, thyme, tarragon, capsicum, lavender and orange, for example.[25] Would there be any difference between being rationed to one per day and being given the whole smell mix every day? Indeed there was. Only one of these options had an effect on memory and on brain cell creation, and that was the one-new-scent-per-day regime. *Novelty* was the key, the researchers concluded.

My excitement grew for one very simple reason: novelty, I knew, is one of the key triggers that can cause a release of noradrenaline in the brain. Like the challenge of the bend in the road, novel experiences wake you up, raise your pulse and dilate your pupils.[26] This was the arousal whose effects on the brain I had been studying for the last thirty years. And now these French researchers were suggesting that the incredible brain-protecting effects of stimulation might happen via exposure to new experiences.

The French researchers went one important step further. They knew that novelty and noradrenaline were twin sisters, so they gave another group of mice the same new-smell-each-day treatment, but they *blocked* noradrenaline in their brains using a noradrenaline antagonist. Sure enough, the novelty-stimulation lost its effects, showing that noradrenaline was critical to how new smells affected the mice's brains.

Then I discovered that some Japanese researchers at the University of Tsukuba in Japan had already discovered a link between enriched environments and noradrenaline.[27] Noradrenaline alone, not other chemical messengers in the brain, increased when mice were kept in enriched, interesting environments – which, as I now knew from the French research, benefited their brains because of all the new experiences the animals had in these rich environments.

Whatever it is that explains the dementia-protective effects of education, mental stimulation and social networks, we call cognitive reserve. Many animal studies, I discovered, showed that noradrenaline may be a key element in cognitive reserve. I was getting closer to explaining why cognitive reserve could reduce dementia: the mice that were exposed to enriched environments and novel smells every day had boosted mental capacity in the short term, and the mechanism by which this was done was mini 'hits' of noradrenaline that were triggered by being exposed to new experiences.

The question I needed to ask now, though, was why would these mini 'hits' of noradrenaline that boost mental sharpness in the short term have any long-term effects on dementia?

In searching for the answer to this question I found out something quite remarkable. Noradrenaline in moderate doses seems to act as a sort of wonder drug to the brain. If you bathe certain other brain cells in noradrenaline – for instance, cholinergic cells, which are important in memory – they survive longer. Not only that, but if you take cells surrounded by the brain-cell-killing amyloid protein and bathe them in noradrenaline, they become less toxic to the brain cells[28] – noradrenaline, in other words, may act like a partial 'antidote' to a key agent of Alzheimer's disease.[29]

And it goes on: noradrenaline, it turns out, is a *neuromodulator* – meaning that it helps the brain learn better by raising its ability to make new connections, hence boosting learning and memory. It is, in other words, like a 'brain fertilizer' and it also helps produce other such fertilizer-like substances.

I collected all this evidence in the paper I was writing about noradrenaline, cognitive reserve and Alzheimer's disease.[30] The noradrenaline hypothesis of dementia – that this 'wonder drug' was being produced naturally in our brains as a result of environmental factors like novelty and mental stimulation – wasn't going to be laughed out of court quite yet.

Nevertheless, almost all of this work was being done in animals – so was it also relevant to human beings? I wondered. You can measure noradrenaline in the mouse brain, but you can't stick probes into a human brain to measure it there. But maybe you can do something else, I thought.

The great thing about science is how sometimes one part of your research becomes relevant to another, apparently unrelated, fragment. In Chapter 1 I explained how we had discovered a way of measuring noradrenaline activity in the brain through the narrowing and widening of the eye's pupil. This part of my research had nothing to do with dementia, which was a quite different and much later direction in research that I had taken. We had discovered the pupil–noradrenaline link because we wanted to understand attention, not dementia. But suddenly these two disconnected domains of my research had come together.

Here was where I had got to. The animal enrichment research was convincing but I didn't know whether it applied to humans. Specifically, I wanted to test whether mental challenge or social networks (the human equivalent of 'enrichment' in animals) had anything to do with noradrenaline, the way it clearly had in animals. If this were the case, it could explain why those Chicago citizens who had strong social networks or were more mentally stimulated were cognitively sharper, and why an educated

Swedish twin is less likely to suffer from dementia than his/her less educated sibling.

Thanks to our attention research, I could now answer these questions because we now had a way of measuring noradrenaline in the human brain. In science, it's often the case that if you look carefully you'll discover that someone else has already tested your bright idea. This was the case when I searched whether any of the ingredients of cognitive reserve affect noradrenaline and I did this by delving into the research on pupil dilation.

Take IQ. I already knew that intelligence, which is heavily linked to educational level, is a very potent ingredient in resilience against dementia. So, does IQ have any linkage to noradrenaline? To my delight, I found not only that it does, but that the link is strong. When we face challenges, our brains release noradrenaline to help sharpen our perception and decision-making processes. I and my colleagues had already discovered that you can measure this by watching the pupils of the eye grow wider: we had validated this against activity in a tiny sliver of brain tissue called the locus coeruleus, which is the source of noradrenaline in the brain.[31] And, as I also showed in Chapter 1, when we are faced with a challenge – whether it be mastering a bend on a fast road or solving a difficult problem – our pupils dilate because our brains are releasing noradrenaline.

Researchers in many institutions around the world, however, had been using pupil dilation as an index of mental effort for many decades, without having our evidence that this reflects noradrenaline activity. So I looked back at this research with new eyes – and what I found was remarkable.

Presented with difficult problems to solve – similar to the sort used in intelligence tests – people of average intelligence widen their pupils when given a mental challenge. This is a familiar finding. But what happens to those with higher than average IQs? Their pupils dilate *much more*, showing that their brains are producing more noradrenaline in response to the challenging problem.[32] Smarter people produce more noradrenaline than less smart people.

But it gets even more interesting. As the problems become tougher, the pupil dilations of average IQ individuals flat-line – they widened roughly the same amount whatever the difficulty. But in those with higher IQ, their pupil dilations ramp up in line with the difficulty of the problem – showing that their brains are steadily rising to the challenge by releasing more and more noradrenaline in accordance with the difficulty of the problems.[33]

I was pretty excited. When people with high IQ are given a challenging problem, their brains produce more noradrenaline than those with lower IQ presented with the same problem. And this noradrenaline is none other than that naturally occurring 'wonder drug' that is both an antidote to amyloid proteins and also strengthens brains with new cells and connections. There was already a proven link between dementia risk and IQ, and also one between noradrenaline and dementia. But there had been a third missing link in this trio – between IQ and noradrenaline. I had just, I *think* for the first time, managed to close it.

And so I found myself proposing a 'noradrenergic theory of cognitive reserve', which was the title of the paper I wrote on the subject which appeared in the journal *Neurobiology of Aging* in digital version in the summer of 2012.[34] This theory proposed that the protective effects of cognitive reserve arose from the strengthening of brain connections and the growth of brain networks, arising from the beneficial effects of a life-time of millions of mini-infusions of noradrenaline, triggered by millions of mental challenges, social interactions and memories retrieved. There was also the intriguing possibility that these repeated noradrenaline surges, providing they did not go beyond their tipping point into severe stress, *may* not only strengthen brain networks, but perhaps affect the disease itself.

I had gone out on a limb with this noradrenergic theory but still there was no direct evidence to support it. And an untestable hypothesis is a useless hypothesis, hence my feeling of anxiety as I published the paper. Studying living human beings and their diseases can be very complex, particularly when you are dealing with changes that happen over many years: these studies themselves take many years to complete and can cost a lot of money.

To test the noradrenergic hypothesis properly, I would have had to recruit 100–200 elderly people and visit them every year to carry out an extensive cognitive assessment until they died. There would then have to have been post-mortem studies of their brains to look for any signs of disease and also to measure the locus coeruleus. My rough estimate was that this would have taken a team of people between seven and ten years to complete and would have cost at least a million euros. Was publishing my hypothesis without any empirical back-up just empty theorizing? I wondered in my darker moments.

Then, one morning in February 2013, an email popped into my inbox from Peter Murphy, a former PhD student of mine working at Leiden University in Holland, who had taken the lead in our experiments showing that pupil dilation reflects noradrenaline activity. 'A paper from Chicago which gives pretty strong support to your noradrenaline hypothesis has just appeared,' he wrote, attaching a link to a newly published digital version of the paper in the journal *Neurology*.[35]

You could have knocked me over with a brain cell.

The Chicago team had done precisely the study that I had wanted to do but thought wasn't feasible in terms of either time or money. They had already collected all the data needed to test my hypothesis as part of a large longitudinal study of ageing. So it would be easy for them to test it on their existing data.

Robert Wilson and his colleagues had followed up 165 elderly people every year until they died an average of just under six years later, at an average age of eighty-eight. Because they had been assessed every year, their decline in cognitive ability could be plotted and compared with the state of their brains assessed after death. Incredibly from my point of view, not only did the researchers detect how much disease was in their brains, they also *counted* the number of cells in each of the so-called 'brainstem nuclei'. These are tiny factories which each produce a different chemical messenger essential to the brain's activity – and one of these, the locus coeruleus, is the noradrenaline factory.

This is what the Chicago team concluded: 'Higher density of noradrenergic neurons in the locus coeruleus was associated with reduced cognitive decline even after accounting for common neurodegenerative lesions in these nuclei and elsewhere in the brain.'[36] In other words, they found that the ability of the brain to produce noradrenaline on its own strongly predicted how fast the mental abilities of a group of people in their eighties would decline over the next six years. And they had showed that this *wasn't* because of a third factor, disease, causing both the decline and the low number of brain cells. Noradrenaline, they concluded, contributed directly to cognitive reserve. Result!

Then, in late 2015, another research group, this time in San Diego, California, also confirmed the link between cognitive reserve and the size of the noradrenaline-producing locus coeruleus among people ranging in age from 56 to 75.[37]

So here was my proposed solution to the puzzling link between education and risk of dementia. Educated people are more likely to encounter mentally challenging problems that cause noradrenaline production, and, what's more, when faced with these problems they produce more noradrenaline than do less educated people. In part because of this process, education builds a bigger, better-connected brain that can keep functioning longer in the face of disease. Noradrenaline is a brain-enhancing, disease-combating chemical that is released in tiny doses hundreds of millions of times over a lifetime. The release happens every time someone is faced with a mental challenge or a novel situation, all the more so for better educated people with higher IQs. So long as challenge doesn't turn into stress and take them beyond the top of their Yerkes–Dodson curve, their brains will benefit from this repeated, brain-enhancing infusion.

Dealing with other people can be the most demanding type of mental challenge we face. Trying to work out what they are feeling and thinking, and responding accordingly, is probably one of the most difficult feats for the human brain. So it is not surprising that social networks also offer protection. I couldn't find any direct evidence that social interaction causes pupils to dilate, but there is plenty of evidence to show that when we see people we like our pupils do indeed swell in size: it therefore seems very likely that human affection boosts the noradrenaline system and so also contributes to cognitive reserve. Good neighbours, friends and family are also brain builders and disease busters, it seems.

My theory led me to a strong prediction about something that every single one of us will have to face up to at some point in our lives – *retirement*. If mental challenge builds brains through noradrenaline release, then anything that diminishes that challenge should do the opposite. Where retirement strips you of mental challenge, then your mental abilities should decline, I reasoned and should also increase your risk of dementia. But was there any evidence for this daunting proposition? What I discovered was sobering.

Countries vary enormously in what proportion of sixty- to sixty-four-year-olds are in work compared to fifty- to fifty-four-year-olds. The difference in proportions is particularly large in countries that have generous early retirement plans, such as France and Italy, where those in their sixties are far less likely still to be working than in the UK or the US. Let's call this the young–old work ratio. It turns out that countries also differ in how much cognitively sharper fifty-year-olds are than sixty-somethings. Let's call this the young–old mental sharpness ratio.

When I looked at the data I discovered that these two ratios are linked: the bigger the proportion of older to younger men who are not working, the larger the young–old mental sharpness ratio.[38] But what is really remarkable about this is that it applies across so many different countries. Take the USA, for instance. Here, roughly 30 per cent fewer sixty- to sixty-four-year-old men are in work compared to fifty- to fifty-four-year olds. In France, thanks to generous pension provision, the same figure is almost *90* per cent. It's probably not a coincidence, then, that sixty-something Americans are on average only 5 per cent less sharp than their fifty-something compatriots. French sixty-somethings, on the other hand, are 20 per cent less sharp on average. French men, in other words, on average lose around 20 per cent of their mental edge between their fifties and their sixties, and American men only 5 per cent. Earlier retirement in France seems to be the most likely culprit.

This doesn't just apply to men. If you calculate what percentage of sixty- to sixty-four-year-old men *and* women are not in paid work in a particular country, then you get similar results. In the USA, for instance, this figure is around 50 per cent, while in France again it is nearly 90 per cent. Sixty- to sixty-four-year-old American men and women score on average eleven out of twelve on a test of cognitive abilities, while in France they only score around eight, on average. Sweden, Switzerland, UK and Denmark have a similar pattern to the USA, while Italy, Belgium and Austria are similar to France.

Retirement may seem a very nice prospect for some, especially if their jobs have been stressful or unpleasant. But there is, it would appear, a potential cost: stopping working may strip you of challenge and hence dull you cognitively. Of course, there are many alternatives to work for creating challenge, but the lesson for me was that if you care about your mental abilities, you should plan to replace work challenges with pretty stimulating non-work demands on your brain after you retire.

But do these changes in cognitive ability really *matter*, you might ask. So what if my memory is a bit poorer, if I am having a great time? The evidence strongly suggests that it probably does matter, because your memory and mental abilities are part of your cognitive reserve and we need plenty of this to boost our chances of avoiding dementia. In France, for instance, there is a good national pension scheme for self-employed people. People who wait until they are sixty-five before availing themselves of it have a roughly 15 per cent lower risk of dementia than those who take their pension at sixty.[39]

Now I had no doubt: mental challenge matters very much indeed, and the right amount of challenge can make you smarter. There is, of course, the problem of stress, which arises when we are pushed beyond our arousal tipping point: then, noradrenaline levels become too high and damaging stress hormones like cortisol flood the brain and body. So mental challenge should ideally take you up to the top of the arousal inverted U-curve – but not beyond it.

In the last chapter I discovered that challenge and stress share a very similar set of bodily feelings but that your mindset can transform one into the other. While challenge smartens you, stress can dull you. We can define stress as where the demands that are being put upon you outstrip your belief in your ability to cope with them. People who suffer from chronic feelings of severe stress on average have worse memory and cognitive function[40,41] than those who don't. What's more, people with chronic, severe stress have an increased risk of dementia.[42]

Stress, then, seems to sap our cognitive reserve, rather than boost it. So where is the line between challenge and stress? Is there such a thing as good stress?

Good Stress

'Good stress' sounded like an oxymoron to me, but then I thought about the evidence that certain types of stresses may improve cognitive function in older people. Yet I also knew that stress saps cognitive reserve. How could I square this circle?

One obvious factor is degrees of stress. Really bad things – losing a child, for instance – could crush you. And, yes, some stresses are so intense that they will scar you, leaving you weaker, not stronger. But setting aside such extreme stresses, different people react to the same stress in different ways, some seeing it as a threat and others as a challenge to be overcome. How could you tell who would react in which way, I wondered?

I scoured the published research for an answer to this. One crucial factor jumped out at me, and at once I remembered a famous kidnapping.

On 11 April 1986, Irishman Brian Keenan walked through the early morning sunshine of Beirut, Lebanon, heading towards the university where he was teaching English. An old Mercedes ran slowly by him, stopped and its door swung open, blocking his path. Four men with guns got out and forced him into the back seat of the car. The car took off and Keenan was ordered down on to the floor: 'I could not, would not go down on the floor amongst their feet. I simply bowed my head, resting it on one of the men's knees. This seemed to cause much confusion,' Keenan later wrote.

So Keenan began four and a half years of brutal captivity in the hands of Islamic Jihad, first alone and then with British journalist hostage John McCarthy. One day Keenan was sitting blindfolded when a guard came in and laid something on the bed beside him. 'New clothes, new clothes, put on,' the voice said. 'No, I will not wear these clothes . . . I will not wear the clothes of a prisoner . . .' Keenan replied.[43]

These two small acts of resistance were perfect examples of what I had discovered in the research as being a key factor in whether someone reacts to stress as a threat or a challenge – as something that diminishes you . . . or makes you stronger.

That something was *control*.

From the very first moment of his kidnapping, Brian Keenan insisted, in the face of threats to his life, on maintaining some control even in the bleakest of regimes of captivity. Instinctively he knew that carving a tiny bit of control out of a situation of complete helplessness was essential for his emotional survival. Prison regimes do all they can to stamp out any such control, because ultimately all prisons work only if they also manage to build prison walls inside their inmates' heads. Keenan refused to let them erect these walls inside his mind.

Keenan suffered a lot of stress in captivity but he coped with it and survived to write one of the most acclaimed hostage memoirs of all time – *An Evil Cradling*. His sheer determination to keep some control over even the tiniest of elements of his prison life was key to the remarkable emotional resilience he showed.

People who believe that they have some control over their lives, no matter what the objective circumstances are, are more likely to see stress as a challenge to face up to, rather than as a threat to retreat from. Individuals vary in how much control they believe they have over their lives. Those who, like Brian Keenan, have a strong sense of internal control answer a firm yes to statements like *I can control many things that are happening in my life* while those with a low sense of control over events endorse statements like *Many events in my life happen by chance.*

When they face stressful events, those with a strong sense of internal control produce far less of the stress hormone cortisol than do low-control individuals and so feel less stressed. Remarkably, these constant infusions of cortisol in low-control people over a lifetime lead to a shrinkage of the hippocampus memory centres in their brains, because in high doses cortisol is toxic for the brain cells there. Their brains, in other words, are *literally weakened* by stress, all because they don't believe that they have much control in their lives.[44]

Brian Keenan's supremely stressful situation, and the objectively tiny amount of control he had over it, illustrates what the research shows, namely that what we are dealing with here is our *attitudes* to stress and control much more than their *objective* nature.

It seems, then, that if 'what doesn't kill me makes me stronger' is to apply to individuals, they must feel some sense of control over events in their lives, even if that control is limited, as was the case in Brian Keenan's small acts of resistance against his captors. Stress, it seems, can only ever be 'good' for someone when they retain *some* control.

Fatalism and Nietzsche don't mix well because fatalistic belief that you can't control events will make you much more stressed by tough times. That stress will sap your ability to cope and in the long term may even deplete the mental abilities you need to solve the problems you face. It will, in short, drain your reservoir of brain-protecting cognitive reserve.

Feeling that you have some control, on the other hand, not only reduces your stress levels, but it does so by helping you cope in a very special way, which I had seen happening in Mark, the badly beaten security guard I had treated years before. Mark had recovered to a large extent because he had mentally 'reappraised' what had made him so stressed. He had reworked in his mind his traumatic experiences, learning to see his anger as anxiety and not to take the attack as something personal to him. Mark could only go through this pretty tough and prolonged mental reworking because he had come to believe that he had some control over his life and his emotions. Without that sense of control, he would not have seen the point of going through the pain and effort of this.

But here is the crucial point in relation to cognitive reserve: this sort of mental reworking means intense and prolonged activity in the frontal lobes of the brain.[45] And this turns down the stress-linked activity in one of the brain's main emotion centres, the amygdala. So by 'reappraising' the stressful events, Mark had not only managed to turn down his anxious and angry emotions, he was also exercising the frontal lobes of his brain.

If you feel more in control of things, I reasoned, then you will be more likely to go to the effort of trying to rework bad, stressful events in your mind. This constant reworking makes you use your frontal lobes – similar to the sort of 'cognitive enrichment' that I had discovered helps older people maintain their mental sharpness. I was excited. Could it be that certain types of stress force those of us with a sense of control into a type of mental activity that enriches our cognitive abilities? Are older people who remember being abused as children more inclined to reflect on their lives and what had happened to them, constantly trying to make sense of it? And does this repeated exercising of the frontal lobes of their brains act as a sort of cognitively enriching stimulation against a backdrop of emotional trauma?

Another factor might be this: reworking these terrible events causes repeated surges of emotion, particularly anger and anxiety. Is it possible that such repeated injections of noradrenaline caused by these emotional surges in some people have some protective effects on the brain and its cognitive functions, albeit in the context of much more severe health and emotional problems which abuse causes?

Imagine I ask you to plunge your hand into a bucket of icy water and hold it there. People find the pain of the cold stressful, but, amazingly, if I ask you to learn a list of words with your hand in the water, you will *remember them better* than under normal circumstances. Your memory *improves* because the stress boosts cortisol and noradrenaline levels and these in turn temporarily boost recall, providing they don't tip you beyond the optimal arousal peak.[46] Some stress, in other words, can make us mentally sharper.

Early in this chapter I found that people in their seventies who endured some types of stresses – the serious illness of their partner, or conflict with family or neighbours – were cognitively sharper than those who hadn't. Other, very bad stresses – like the death of a child or a grandchild – had no such protective effect.

I realized at once what might explain this: you have some control over how to look after a partner who has had a stroke and also in trying to sort out conflict in your family. But there is nothing you can do about the death of a child or grandchild – here there is no control and hence no upside to the stress. Dealing with illness or conflict, on the other hand, may force you to use your frontal lobes to solve new problems and manage your emotions by constantly having to 'reappraise' the situation and your own actions. The emotional surges may, if not too severe, also raise noradrenaline levels and hence strengthen cognitive networks in the brain.

To call such stresses 'benign' would be stretching things. For your life partner to suffer a stroke is miserable and stressful. And conflict within the family is painful. But these stresses can force you to up your mental game and so have a potentially benign side to them. They are definitely challenging and challenge – if you have the right mindset – is brain-enhancing because it forces your brain into an active mode which is cognitively enriching.

So, could it be that the challenge of trying to come to terms with early sexual abuse stimulated those people who had suffered it into a lifetime of mental activity which, though emotionally gruelling, had a small through entirely insufficient silver lining of boosted mental sharpness?

Sexual abuse at an early age sentences most people to a lifetime of self-exploration in an attempt to come to terms with what has happened at a time of life when personality is being formed. The experience of abuse can embed itself in the developing self and it can take many decades of thinking, emotional turmoil, conversations and counselling to free the self and personality of this alien intrusion. This is like a massive rewriting of the software of the self and it is a job that for many is never finished. But a possible, albeit entirely inadequate, consolation here is that this is virtually non-stop rethinking that, as outlined in the last chapter, takes place in the frontal lobes of the brain. This constant exercising of the frontal lobe self-awareness and self-reflection systems may act as a powerful sort of mental stimulation that may trigger repeated noradrenaline release over the years and so have this positive effect on cognitive function. Mental working through terrible experiences may, in other words, provide a sort of cognitive enrichment for some victims, though for many others there is not even this meagre crumb of benefit against the awfulness of a lifetime's suffering.

So, yes, what doesn't kill me *can* make me cognitively stronger and being cognitively stronger will, in turn, make me a better problem solver and so a better coper with stress, provided I have some sense of control over my life. Problems that challenge us can act as a type of mental stimulation that make our brains give multiple 'fixes' of the powerful chemical noradrenaline, building our cognitive reserve and so giving us the mental strength to solve new problems better. This, of course, depends on the challenges lifting us up to a peak of performance and not tilting us beyond it: because, as I find out in the next chapter, too much stress for too long does certainly not strengthen us.

Joanne's phone call had set me on a journey where I discovered that sometimes, for some people, stressful experiences can mentally sharpen them. But what about the opposite? Is it possible to have *too many* of the good things in life, or *too little* stress, I wondered.

6

Can Too Much Happiness Be Bad for You?

I heard the hoarse cry, *'No! Get back!'*, my hands clawing at the dashboard and feet pumping reflexively at the floor – before understanding that the shout was mine.

Wide-eyed and heart pumping, I wrenched my eyes from the road ahead to look desperately at my colleague Ken, who was driving. He was smiling. Smiling!

I shouted again, *'Stop!'*

The flimsy Renault leaned shakily into the long, blind curve at the far limits of its stability . . . and on the wrong side of the road. A high stone wall whipped by in the periphery of my vision and I knew we had seconds before we were going to be hit by the next vehicle to come round the blind bend.

The imminence of death drew a third desperate shout out of me that seemed, finally, to get through to Ken. He raised his foot from the accelerator and jerked the car in a crazy, heart-stopping swerving path back to the proper side of the road.

'Let. Me. Drive!' I panted through gritted teeth. Ken, no longer smiling, pulled in. He stepped out into the cold Scottish twilight and let me take over. By the time we reached our destination, his air of wild, exhilarated abandon had dissipated and I could sense him sinking into a state of morose agitation.

The last time I had been in a vehicle with Ken it was in the ambulance that was taking him to hospital, sometime in late 1981. I found myself sitting on a bed in the back with one of the crew while Ken sat up front with the driver, directing him with hilarious, rapid-fire quips towards the hospital.

I have a few other transport-related memories of Ken. One is of him appearing at a party and ushering everyone outside to see the gleaming, bright red sports car that he had bought hours before. We all blanched as he boasted that he had driven the twenty miles from the showroom to the party in under ten minutes.

Another memory is of the sudden disappearance of the red sports car, rumoured to have been repossessed, and the appearance of the tinny little Renault in which I was subsequently to see my life flashing before my eyes.

The last memory I have is of Ken's Renault sitting, dusty and undriven, outside a house from which he had been extracted on another day by another ambulance. But this time with no quips and no restless exuberance – he was a wordless shell of a human being, stooped and looking neither to right nor left as he was led from his house to the waiting ambulance.

Ken suffered from bipolar disorder – a very clear case of this illness. He had enormous swings of mood from ecstatic exuberance and overconfidence to mute depression when he would lie hunched and unmoving in his bed for day upon day, week upon week, until someone called an ambulance to take him to hospital.

When Ken was 'on the way up' he was brilliant company, fantastically witty and a superb professional dedicated to his job. He was also an inspiring leader, focused on goals and able to bring people together to achieve them. His exuberance was infectious and you felt uplifted in his company.

But as Ken's mood continued up, things would become more difficult. He would start feeling super-human, all-powerful and super-optimistic. No lorry would hit him if he drove too fast on the wrong side of the road; no bank would deny him the funds for anything he wanted; and no achievement was beyond him. There were no downsides, no risks, no anxiety in Ken's hyper-exuberant world.

Ken was muscled and strong. One day he grabbed me round the neck in an affectionate hug, laughing and joking. I felt myself choking, but couldn't speak because of the pressure. He was oblivious to this – his self-awareness had diminished to a point where he was living in a cocoon of ecstasy with no remaining shred of self-monitoring for mistakes or risks. My hands were tearing at his flexed, iron-hard arm as my vision became blurred and a terrible sensation of suffocation clouded my mind.

Suddenly he released me, laughing at my gasping for breath, unaware of what he had done. Not long after that the ambulance came.

I have never forgotten Ken – in fact, even though it was more than thirty years since I had seen him, he came into the forefront of my mind as I searched for the last piece of the Nietzsche jigsaw. I'll return to how he helped me find it at the end of the chapter. First, I have to tell you about one of my earliest patients.

Joe

There was something about Joe's demeanour that I couldn't quite put my finger on. Tall and handsome, the twenty-two-year-old draped himself across the chair in the languorous way that could be mistaken for insolent self-confidence. But there wasn't much self-confidence on show here. I couldn't figure him out. Then it came to me – it was as if the air had been sucked out of him, leaving this *absence* – but of what? Energy, drive, I quickly realized. He had the air of a young man who felt defeated without ever having been in a fight.

Joe wasn't terribly clear about why he had come to see me. Gradually it emerged that it was his mother and stepfather who had urged him to 'see someone'. I was that someone, but it was not too clear to me either why he was there. Gradually I teased Joe's story out of him: his languorous manner was not confined to his posture – his language was similarly draped and empty of movement, full of 'aahs' and 'ehs' and 'sooos' and 'likes'. But slowly, a sort of picture began to emerge.

Joe had had a blessed childhood as the popular, athletic, academically gifted son of doting parents. He also had two admiring younger sisters and a privileged upbringing, enjoying long, carefree summer holidays at the family cottage by the sea. At school he had a group of close friends and won as many athletic trophies as he did academic prizes. He always had money to spend and, when he took a year off to travel, he chose the most exotic, out-of-the-way corners of the Earth from which to send postcards to his admiring friends.

But then a few things happened to Joe – troubles come in threes, they say. When he was nineteen, and in his first year at university, his girlfriend, with whom he had travelled the world, broke off their relationship. A month later, his parents announced that they were separating. And soon after that, for the first time in his life, he failed an exam.

Joe reacted badly to these three unfortunate events. He lost motivation and didn't study over the summer, failing the repeat exam and dropping out of university. His sunny, confident personality changed and he became rather listless, cynical and depressed. He also began to smoke a lot of cannabis and drifted from job to low-grade job, losing contact with his old friends and mixing with a disparate bunch of drifters like the person he was rapidly becoming.

What happened to Joe?

I couldn't quite get my head round Joe. While he didn't seem too clear about what he was feeling or thinking, there was a sense that he had a considerable awareness of himself. Some of us have a very high opinion of ourselves, to the point where we feel a greater sense of entitlement to special treatment from life and from other people, as well as a preoccupation with 'me' and my needs, over those of others. Narcissistic personalities like this can find it hard to cope when life does not deal them the cards they think they deserve. So was Joe a disappointed narcissist, I wondered?

As we talked, this seemed to make some sense, particularly when it occurred to me what a blessed generation Joe belonged to in the late 1970s: he and his contemporaries had no fear of unemployment and were assured of jobs when they left school or college. They had moved from adolescence to early adulthood with a sense that anything was possible and that the limits were few.

I decided to look at the research on psychology and economics, and, indeed, discovered that there are higher levels of narcissism among people who transitioned into adulthood during economic good times. In contrast, those who became adults during a period of recession – around the 2008 crash, for instance – are significantly less prone to narcissistic personality traits.[1]

The wider economic and political environment moulds the personalities of people at this crucial period in their lives when their adult personalities, values and attitudes are being formed.

Tough economic times create people who tend to be more cautious, risk-averse and grateful for what they have got: the challenge of making a living in difficult times means they are less restless and more content with their lot. This goes together with a more 'other-oriented' mindset, in the sense of being more inclined to think about other people – family, friends, teams and colleagues for instance – and less inclined to dwell on their own individual needs, aspirations, disappointments and goals. Good times such as Joe experienced, on the other hand, can breed the opposite – a restless striving for more of the same, and with that a very self-focused, individualistic approach to life shading in more extreme cases into narcissism.[2]

This all seemed to fit with what I knew about Joe. But then I had doubts. So what if Joe was a little narcissistic – why was that making him so miserable and unmotivated?

In the last hundred years there can have been few worse economic times in the Western world than the 1930s – the time of food kitchens, mass unemployment and, in the USA, the dust bowl starvation portrayed in books such as John Steinbeck's *The Grapes of Wrath*. Yet in such a time of economic depression, *psychological* depression among young adults was much, much lower than it was in modern times of prosperity. While the average US college student in 1938 scored quite low on a standard depression questionnaire, the average score on the same measure at the height of Bill Clinton's prosperous nineties was 50 per cent higher than in 1938.[3]

Easy times, then, not only tend to breed narcissistic tendencies in some, they also create more unhappiness. Tough times, on the other hand, don't just breed more grateful, other-minded young adults; for some reason they also make them less depressed, according to the evidence. Perhaps it was the easy times that he had grown up in that had demotivated Joe and made him so unhappy. But *why?* What is it about good times that causes this?

The Grass in the Greenhouse

While driving to the west coast of Ireland in 2012, I was thinking about Joe and feeling a bit stuck when my mind was caught by a voice on the radio – someone talking about, of all things, grass. He was describing how some species survive in tough environments like the Russian steppe where howling gales batter their thin stems flat for days on end, only to spring back up again to resume their growth when the winds die down.

But it wasn't this remarkable feature of nature's engineering design that grabbed me – it was what he said next. 'If you take exactly the same species of grass, grow it in a greenhouse, then plant it out in the open, the first gust of wind will snap it and kill it.'[4]

A gust of wind buffeted the car and the passing trees groaned backwards, flailing against a sudden Atlantic storm: I was approaching the coast, but my mind was filled with something else – the image of that tall, handsome stem of grass growing strong and proud in the warm, still air of its protecting greenhouse. Then the thought crossed my mind – was Joe's early life like that long stem of grass in the greenhouse that snapped as soon as the strong wind of adversity hit him?

As soon as I got back to Dublin I decided to check whether there was any research to back up my speculation about Joe. There was. Researchers at the University of Buffalo had, for instance, asked around two thousand American adults about the extent of difficulties and challenges they had had in their lives[5] – illnesses, injuries, assault, bereavement, severe financial difficulties, disasters like floods, earthquakes or fires and so on. Over three years between 2001 and 2004, they followed them up to ask about their levels of stress, coping with life and general life satisfaction.

I was very surprised to see evidence of another inverted U-curve, but in this case relating adversity and psychological resilience. People with high levels of adversity were stressed, coping badly and had poor life satisfaction – but so were those, like Joe, with *no adversity* in their previous lives. In contrast, those at the peak of an adversity curve, namely people with *moderate* levels of stressful experiences in their lives, were doing very well psychologically compared to the other two groups.

A very similar tipping point exists for ten- to twelve-year-old children who are adopted, I discovered. Those who have had moderate levels of stress before adoption in the USA had much higher stress resilience and were much tougher psychologically than were the natural-born children of upper-middle-class parents who had led the sort of sheltered life that Joe had. Children who had had very tough times before adoption, for instance in poor orphanages, had similarly low levels of resilience to the no-stress US-born children.[6] Nietzsche was right to an extent – what doesn't kill me *does* make me stronger, as long as it is not too severe.

How Do Tough Times Make Resilient People?

Imagine a bucket filled with ice-cold water. I ask you to put your hand into it and hold it there for as long as you can bear it. The ice cubes rattle together as your hand goes in and a freezing band clamps round your forearm. The first shock of the cold gradually transmutes into a throbbing pain. How long can you last?

This is the 'cold pressor test' used to measure how much you can tolerate pain. People who, like Joe, have never known difficult times in their earlier life, pull their hand out of the water much sooner than do those who have had moderately tough times in their past – they can't tolerate physical pain.[7] The same applies to people with too much adversity in their past. So there's a tipping point of 'what doesn't kill you' that makes you mentally stronger – not just for physical pain, but for mental pain like loss and anxiety, too, I guessed.

Millions of people are disabled by chronic low back pain and the ice water test finding applies to them also: people who have never known adversity end up more disabled and stressed by their back pain, and use much more painkiller medication than do people who have had moderate setbacks and difficulties in their lives.[8]

But how does this 'mental toughening' happen? People who have never known adversity tend to get sucked into something called *catastrophizing* about their pain. This means that they think thoughts like 'this pain's going to overwhelm me' and 'I can't stand this'. But if you've ever had to endure a certain amount of mental or physical pain in the past, then you know that you *can* stand it, and that it *doesn't* overwhelm you.

'What doesn't kill you' gives you one crucial lesson: most of the time, bad times come to an end. If you have never learned this lesson, then even small bad things like the pain of your hand in ice water feel like a threat and not just a discomfort: life hasn't dealt the Joes of this world any real psychological or physical pain before, so how can they know otherwise? And feeling out of control because of being 'overwhelmed' by pain is a frightening thought that will ramp up your anxiety and so further sap your toughness in the face of pain.

Here is what I had worked out about adversity, thanks to Joe: so long as it is not too severe, adversity teaches us that bad things will come to an end eventually. It also makes us used to the physical 'arousal' symptoms – racing pulse, sweaty palms, and so on – so we aren't scared by these natural responses to threat.

If some harsh things have happened to you in the past, and you have survived them, then all the thoughts, worries and bodily reactions to stress are familiar to you and – most importantly – you know that eventually they will go back to normal. It is the psychological equivalent of a vaccination against a disease: your body is exposed to weakened or dead bacteria or viruses so that it can then build up the antibodies to fight off the real thing.

A Run in Central Park

It was October 2012 and I had recently arrived in the USA to begin a sabbatical. Looking out of the windows of the fourteenth floor of our Upper West Side apartment, I thought that the livid blue flashes around the New York skyline were lightning strikes until I realized that they were spreading from the ground up. Only then did I see that they were the flares of electrical sub-stations exploding as the floodwaters hit them. The old wooden windows of our unrefurbished apartment shuddered and rattled as the whole building seemed to tense bravely like a feisty but frail old lady against every ferocious gust that Superstorm Sandy loosed against it.

The whole southern half of Manhattan was plunged into an apocalyptic darkness, as billions of gallons of sea water slopped and gushed into its subways and buildings. But with our extra fifty feet of elevation further up that crowded island, I sat fully heated and lit, perversely enjoying the storm, my laptop open on my knee as I puzzled over the question that had been put to me on the first day of my sabbatical.

My colleague at Columbia University, Yaakov Stern, with whose group I had come to spend a few months, had coined the term 'cognitive reserve'. As I showed in the last chapter, some elements of cognitive reserve such as education seem to offer some protection against dementia. Yaakov's question was this: were there any particular parts of the brain involved in allowing cognitive reserve to have its protective effects?

Now, more than a month into my stay, I wasn't any nearer to answering the question and a fear that I might be wasting my precious sabbatical niggled at me. That was why I found myself sitting at my computer in the middle of the second most destructive storm in US history. I was working at Yaakov's problem rather than enjoying the wine that I had waited so long for in the pre-storm emergency liquor store queue – incidentally, a line much longer than for any of the food stores. I went to bed with the storm still pounding the city.

The streets were uncannily empty the following day as I set out along West 86th Street for my morning jog in Central Park, just two blocks away. I could see a few fallen trees in the park and found my entrance blocked by a sign saying that the park was closed. But to run around the reservoir of Central Park is the sweetest of experiences which never ceases to give me a thrill and the sense of every day being so precious in that amazing city pushed me into stepping round the sign and into the park.

I was halfway down the east side of the lake, rather missing the usual dense scattering of morning runners – especially the eighty- and ninety-year-olds in which New York specializes – when a figure stepped out in front of me, hand held out. It was a cop with a very forbidding expression on his face.

'You saw the park was closed?'

'Yes.'

'But you came past the sign anyway?'

'Yes.'

My heart was racing – there was something about his manner that made me think he might be about to give me a summons.

'That's an incredibly stupid thing to do.'

I didn't really think it was – only a handful of trees had come down, though I suppose one could have been teetering on some sort of post-storm brink and landed on me – but it seemed far less likely than a piece of debris from a roof falling on me in the streets. But you don't argue with a New York cop.

'Yes, sorry about that.'

He jabbed his thumb towards the east and snarled: 'Get out of the park.'

A mixed basket of emotions accompanied my brisk jog towards the nearest gate – a sense of relief that I had got away without a summons steadily overwhelming the cop-induced anxiety – but strongest of all was an acute sense of embarrassment that I, a white-haired professor, had been caught out and then scolded like a naughty child by a policeman half my age.

As I trotted the long rectangular detour around the park back towards the apartment – I had plenty of time to think during the monotony of the longer-than-usual jog – I began to think about my reaction to my run-in with the policeman.

First there was my pulse, which was beating much faster than usual: the aftermath of the fear that I might be ticketed by a sleep-deprived, grumpy cop. Second, I felt hyper-attentive to everything, as if my brain was scanning for another police-man who might jump out at me. Third, I had a strong sense of unfamiliarity: everything was *new*, including the empty streets, the fallen trees and the unearthly silence of the city.

But there was a fourth thing that overshadowed all of these: my self-consciousness. In the aftermath of the encounter, my mind kept running over the rights and wrongs of my ignoring the sign. In doing so, I could feel my ego engaged in a self-repair operation, attempting to shore up my view of myself as a law-abiding, safety-conscious, responsible, respectable citizen.

By now I was walking down the west side perimeter of the park, my self-conscious agitation gradually being superseded by the inkling of an answer to Yaakov's question. The initial agitation I had felt was a symptom of fear- and embarrassment-induced arousal and, as I well knew, noradrenaline is a key player in these symptoms. Before I came to New York, I had already published a paper proposing the theory that Yaakov's cognitive reserve might be built up by repeated infusions of brain-connection-strengthening noradrenaline in the brain.[9] I also knew that moderate stress may have positive effects on the cognitive function of older people, possibly also via noradrenaline.

In my long, self-conscious walk back to our apartment, I suddenly realized how to answer Yaakov's question: noradrenaline is important for cognitive reserve, so what I must do is find out which are the brain networks in which noradrenaline plays a particularly important role. Safely back home, a little chastened, I showered, breakfasted and set about finding out.

It took me several days and the perusal of scores of studies, but the answer was clear. Noradrenaline is central to four brain networks. First, there is arousal and alertness. Second, attention, particularly sustained attention. Third is response to novelty – unexpected events trigger noradrenaline release in the brain with a vengeance. And the fourth? Self-awareness.[10]

What was remarkable about discovering these was that they were exactly the four elements I had noticed about myself during my chastened return from the park. This minor stress had not only raised my pulse, focused my attention and made everything look rather new and unfamiliar; it had also brought *me*, my *self*, into the focus of my conscious attention. It had made me self-aware – or perhaps self-conscious is a better way of putting it – in quite an uncomfortable way.

I had already come to the conclusion that alertness and arousal are important for the Nietzsche principle to apply (Chapters 1 and 4) and that attention is crucial in strengthening us emotionally (Chapters 2 and 3). Also, that novelty is crucial in building our mental strength through boosting brain connections (Chapter 5). Self-awareness, however, stood out, not only as the only one of these factors which I had not yet considered in relation to finding the Nietzschean tipping point, but, more importantly, it rang loud bells of recognition with regard to the puzzle that Joe presented.

My Relationship with Me

What I hadn't previously been able to put my finger on in Joe's case was this. For all his cool demeanour and apparent world-weariness, it was clear that the one thing that was uppermost in Joe's mind almost 100 per cent of the time was . . . *Joe*. Although he wasn't a full-blown narcissist, Joe, I was fairly certain, was self-absorbed and not in a good way. He gave the impression that he was always watching himself and listening to himself as he spoke. Doing this uses precious mental resources and so Joe's slow and distracted demeanour could very plausibly be explained by his mind being filled with Joe-thoughts.

We all pay attention to ourselves from time to time – I certainly did after meeting the angry cop in Central Park. Before that event, however, my mind had been focused outwards on the stunning Manhattan skyline, and 'me' was only fleetingly on my mind.

With the subways closed in the post-Sandy chaos, and the clean-up crews working on the deserted streets, I settled down at home to find out about the science of self-awareness. The conclusions were clear – if, like Joe, your self is on your mind a lot, generally that will make you feel unhappy and anxious. There is an exception to this in that if you manage to focus your attention only on the positive things about yourself, then dwelling on your assets and achievements actually lifts your mood.[11] But positive self-focus will use up mental space and may make you a tiresome companion.

I was making progress with understanding Joe better, but what about Yaakov's question to me about cognitive reserve? I thought I had put my finger on the cognitive processes involved – arousal, attention, novelty and awareness – and later we discovered that the right half of the brain, particularly the right frontal lobe, was strongly linked to these.[12,13]

So, I had three of the four noradrenaline-linked cognitive functions in the bag – arousal, attention and awareness – that our own and many other studies showed were linked to a network on the right half of the brain, particularly in the right frontal and the right parietal lobes. This, it turned out, was true also for the fourth of the noradrenaline functions – novelty.[14] So, thanks to my humiliating encounter with NYPD in Central Park, I had an answer for Yaakov Stern: the right hemisphere of the brain, particularly the frontal and parietal regions, is an excellent candidate for a cognitive reserve network. And it seemed to me that these processes that built resilience against dementia were also good candidates for resilience in the face of stressful experiences.

Rethinking 'Me'

Joe didn't seem able to reconcile the conflict between the old, ideal, successful Joe and the current – in his eyes at least – unsatisfactory Joe. How could he do this other than by accepting who he was now and forgetting who he had once been?

I have seen many people who have had to come to terms with much more dramatic changes in 'me' than Joe faced. Some were clever, handsome young men and women with vibrant social lives and great careers ahead of them who suddenly found themselves brain-damaged in an accident, then unemployed and cut off from their herd, their lives in reverse as they found themselves living back at home with elderly parents.

Others were family men and women cut down in their prime by a stroke or some other neurological condition that, in the blink of an eye, altered them from being the dominant figures in their families and communities to being totally dependent on others for their care.

How do people cope with a level of stress that makes Joe's look trivial in comparison? I saw many people surrender to a sort of resigned passivity. A few others were angry and resentful, tormenting themselves and their loved ones with a rage against what they saw as the unfairness of it all. Some – like Paul in Chapter 3 – had a strange equanimity about their sudden disability, as if it didn't bother them, but this, I only now realize, was because the self-awareness parts of their brains had been damaged by stroke or head injury.

But there was a fourth, smaller group of people who seemed to have found something positive in the terrible losses they had suffered. These, it seemed to me, were the ultimate exemplars of 'what doesn't kill me, makes me stronger'. Gerry was one who sticks in my mind. He had been an engineer on an industrial site when a piece of concrete had fallen on him, leaving him severely brain-damaged and unable to work. His self-awareness was not affected, however, and he went through months of intense grief and depression after he came out of his initial coma and started to confront his difficulties in the world. He was bitterly aware that his awkward, halting speech and limping gait were steadily disconnecting him from his former professional friends.

But, gradually, Gerry seemed to come to terms with the new realities of his life. He became more relaxed and less focused on what he couldn't do any more. Instead, he started to talk about how he had begun to paint – something he could never do in the past. He started to paint vividly coloured pictures that had a child-like intensity and even a sort of naïve genius to them; the more he immersed himself in his art, the faster his depression lifted.

Gerry was one of a group of my former patients who found something positive emerging from their terrible disabilities. What hadn't killed them really had made them emotionally stronger. But as I thought about these people, I realized that, to find that strength, two things have to be in place. The first is a capacity for honest self-awareness: only if you are clear-minded in seeing the new limitations in who you are and what you can do can you then make the changes needed. This is almost always very painful and very hard and it took Gerry almost two years to give up wishing to be as he used to be.

The second critical ingredient for finding the positive among the terrible is the sheer grit of 'going on' that I discussed in Chapter 3 – that determined 'approach' towards getting through tough times even though you aren't sure what goal you are heading to, other than the goal of simply 'going on'. Gerry had to force himself into approach mode and try out painting: he was desperate with the isolation and boredom of living on his own at home with no job and few social outlets. Gerry had both self-awareness and the ability to go on, but, while Joe had plenty of self-awareness, he hadn't learned to *go on*.

There is always the risk of sounding like Pollyanna when telling stories like Gerry's, but his type of story is not just anecdote – research bears it out, I discovered. Take the case of paralysing spinal injuries – what is the emotional state of paraplegics and quadriplegics a year or more after the disabling injury? To answer that question you have to ask – compared to whom?

Ideally, you should contrast them with a group that has also experienced a single dramatic event that changed their lives beyond recognition. Researchers in Illinois had the brilliant idea of using *lottery winners* as the control group and tracked down twenty-two of them to compare with twenty-nine people paralysed by spinal injury. Here was the surprising finding – a year after their life-changing experiences, the two groups got *the same* amount of enjoyment from the everyday pleasures of life.[15]

Meanwhile, a colleague in Oxford, Joanna Collicutt, had studied individuals with Gerry's type of problem, traumatic brain injury, interviewing one group just seven months after their injury and another roughly ten years beyond their accident. She was interested in whether any of them showed signs of so-called 'post-traumatic growth', namely the perception of positive consequences coming out of the terrible injury of the type that Gerry showed.

She indeed found that many said that there were such positives, with comments like: 'I appreciate every day', 'I feel a sense of closeness with others', 'I feel I am more self-reliant' and 'I have developed new interests'. One woman even told the researchers that one of the best things that had ever happened to her was her brain injury (the other was divorcing her first husband!).[16]

Collicutt's patients were perfect examples of Nietzsche's maxim – what hadn't killed them had indeed made them stronger. They had learned, like the Illinois paraplegics, to take pleasure in the small things in life, and to change how they saw and assessed themselves, giving up standards that no longer applied, like success in their career, earning capacity and social status.

It's not easy to give up these benchmarks for your self-esteem, though. It took years for Gerry to stop feeling a sense of loss about his career, his income and his social circle and to begin to feel good about himself as a painter and as a person who takes pleasure in the everyday moments of life. The only way to do this is by being aware of yourself, and in particular by 'reappraisal' of what has happened to you. As I delved into this process – one that every one of us has to do eventually – I found out that there are two different ways in which you can reappraise what has happened to you. You can reappraise your situation, or you can also reappraise your *self*.

Here is a *situation* example: you meet your colleague at the water-cooler and he bites your head off for some innocent remark you make. This makes you feel anxious, angry and unsettled. But then you think, 'Ah, I bet he's had a lousy weekend and is feeling miserable', and immediately you feel a lot better because you have 'reappraised' the situation.

Now here is a *self* example: the same colleague bites your head off and makes you feel very bad. But then you see him immediately afterwards being very jolly and light-hearted with several of your colleagues. You realize that here it is not the situation – it is *you*. You haven't done anything to upset him that you know of and when you ask him he agrees that you've done nothing, but none the less he continues to behave in the same very negative way.

In this latter situation you feel a lot worse because rejection by others is the biggest stressor known to humankind and there are good reasons for this. In our evolutionary past, being rejected from the group meant you might be killed by enemies or predators. And social rejection makes us feel pain that switches on exactly the same brain networks as physical pain – indeed, it even feels a little better if you take an aspirin![17]

So your colleague has, without explanation, rejected you and it is causing you a lot of stress and anxiety. And the main source of that stress is the question that it puts in your mind: 'Maybe there is something wrong with *me*.' Your precious *self* is under major threat and you cannot come up with a reappraisal of the *situation* to let you off the hook. That is where self-reappraisal comes in and, with it, the word I had been searching for when thinking about those brave people coming to terms with their terrible losses after brain or spinal injury. That word is *distancing*.

Distancing means taking a step out of the cockpit of the self. When I am relaxed and happy, and maybe in a playful but reflective frame of mind, I can sometimes play at detaching a little from myself – maybe laughing at myself a bit, or ironically observing my own idiosyncrasies. That is distancing. But things are different when my self is under threat, say, under public criticism by a rival at a business meeting – no way am I climbing out of that cockpit. Instead, I go into full emergency drill to protect it, anxiously scanning for possible damage to its fuselage in case it will crash. No distancing here, no playful detachment, but full-on anxious self-awareness that disturbs my sleep and preoccupies my waking day. Just like Joe.

Self-reappraisal is hard to do but if you practise you can get better at it. It means climbing out of the cockpit of the self for a short while, which is possible only because the human brain has this remarkable ability to *watch itself watching*.

Self-reappraisal means accepting the reality of what has happened. My colleague, for reasons he will not explain, does not like me any more – but I can reappraise my self to change the impact of that reality so that it becomes less of a threat. For example, I can say to myself that I have lots of other colleagues who like me and that it is not my problem if he has behaved so inconsistently. Distancing is only one method – but it is a very powerful one that reduces the distress in people coping with tough times.[18] Maybe you have been told that you are just about to lose your job, for instance. It makes sense to worry about practical things like money and survival, but you don't *have* to let the imminent loss of your job become an even bigger source of anxiety by letting it become a threat to your *self*.

I guessed that many of my old patients who had devastating disabilities had survived emotionally by learning to look at themselves in a slightly distanced way, perhaps reappraising with thoughts like '*I* am not my job', '*I* am not my sexual abilities', '*I* am not my legs' . . . and so on.

I felt that I now understood something quite profound about 'post-traumatic growth'. It involves both withdrawal *and* approach. Yes, you need to 'go on' in the face of loss, but first you have to pull back from the old goals of your old self. Being strengthened by what doesn't kill you, then, means deploying both the right and the left sides of your brain in a way that, I suddenly realized, must lead to a more complicated emotional state than simple happiness.

This tallied with Joanna Collicutt's finding. Her patients who showed the most post-traumatic growth after their brain injuries also *felt the most anxiety*,[19] precisely that complicated combination of emotions that lay behind the strengthening that Nietzsche envisaged.

This mix of emotions is far from simple, and maybe can never be completely comfortable. But perhaps it is this very *edginess* that can make many people who have been strengthened by what doesn't kill them feel so alive. It does so, I guessed, by drawing on the positivity and goal focus of the left frontal lobe network combined with the watchful, detached and slightly anxious self-awareness of the right.

The research supports this view, I discovered: while rethinking a *situation* (my colleague had a bad weekend) tends to activate the left frontal lobe, *self*-reappraisal (distancing myself from the pain of being disliked) switches on right frontal lobe regions.[20,21] This delicate balance between approach and avoidance that underpins our ability to become stronger in the face of terrible setbacks also plays out in the brain.

The Tipping Point of Self

I opened this chapter describing Ken, who nearly killed me on a Scottish road. In Ken I could see, played out in extreme form, this struggle between approach and avoidance in his brain. It was Ken's tragedy that he could seldom find the balance between these two extremes. When he did, it was a true finely balanced tipping point – he was a remarkably talented and attractive human being but, unfortunately, he never seemed to be able to stay in the zone for long.

In the upswings of bipolar disorder, as we might expect, the left frontal lobe of the brain is highly active, contributing to the forward-looking, goal-hungry exuberance of the fired-up, go-getting, outward-facing leader. When in the downswing of depression, the right frontal lobe dominates, with its anxiety, inhibition, withdrawal and pessimistic preoccupation with risk, error and failure.[22]

Joe was not suffering from bipolar disorder, but he was stuck in a mild but chronic zone of avoidance, low mood, anxiety and self-preoccupation. He needed to move closer to the balanced zone which, had he reached it, he would have found much easier to maintain than poor Ken.

As I remembered Ken, it confirmed my conclusion that to become stronger after bad things happen, what you need to find is a *balance*. Not just a balance between approach and avoidance, optimism and pessimism, reward-seeking and punishment avoidance, but a balance – a tipping point – of the *self*, I realized.

When Ken was in his up mode, he was bursting with energy and optimism, but, above all, he was hungry for the *reward* of new goals achieved and pleasures anticipated. When I looked into it, I discovered that people in the up phase of bipolar disorder actually have a highly excitable pleasure centre – part of the reward network – in the so-called ventral striatum part of the brain.[23]

And a super-energized pleasure centre like Ken's is something you see in a different type of person: cocaine users. Cocaine makes you feel exuberant, optimistic and all-powerful, too. Indeed, a number of commentators have speculated that widespread cocaine use by Wall Street and London City bankers and traders may have played a small part in the global financial meltdown of 2008.[24] The office of the infamous fraudster Bernie Madoff was apparently known as 'the North Pole' because of the gargantuan quantities of 'snow' to be found there.[25]

Ken's turbocharged approach motivation broke him financially but at least he couldn't bring down a global financial system. But like the financial cocaine users, his self-awareness was blunted, as was any appreciation of risk – as I found to my cost on that terrifying drive in the Scottish mountains.

But you don't have to be a cocaine user to be locked into a less extreme form of Ken's state of mind. Most of us, from time to time, lock ourselves into a zone of intense focus on day-to-day tasks and goals. Sometimes the zone is one of grinding routine, but in others it can be an eager forward-looking focus on future rewards of promotion, status or financial bonuses.

If you operate too strongly in approach mode, anticipating yet more rewards, inevitably this inhibits your right frontal lobe avoidance system. On the plus side, this also quells your anxiety and lets you 'go on'. One major negative, however, is that it diminishes your self-awareness. You may well know someone who has had a run of success, and it has 'gone to his head', making him appear arrogant, self-centred and careless of other people's interests and feelings.

Perhaps the biggest cost is that you do not continually 'appraise' your self, gradually adjusting it in the face of life's challenges. Self-awareness is crucial to reappraising the self, but if it is dulled by constant reward-seeking, then the self is less likely to 'grow'.

By 'grow', I mean a less dramatic form of personal development than my engineer patient Gerry was forced to undergo, due to his brain injury. Gerry rose to his challenge by discovering that life could have a bitter-sweet tang even if you couldn't work any more, even if you lost most of your old friends, even if your speech was halting and difficult to understand, and even if your limping, shuffling gait drew looks from strangers on the street.

We all, ultimately, have to make adjustments like Gerry's. Everyone reaches a time in their career, sport or romantic life when he or she is no longer ahead of the pack. There can be a dismay at being overtaken by younger models, at no longer being 'top dog'. Some men and women find it very hard to come to terms with the fact that they have lost their youthful looks, while others find it painful to give up the status of a senior position at work. Yet these are trivial challenges compared to what those who are suddenly paralysed from the neck down or brain damaged have to face.

So here, finally, was the solution to the Nietzsche puzzle – to be strengthened by adversity, you have to find a finely balanced tipping point of your self. When bad things happen, whether your self grows or shrinks depends on the struggle between approach and avoidance. Joe's self hadn't grown when he faced tough times – his had shrunk into anxious avoidance and his life was stuck. Gerry had grown, but only after a period of total withdrawal, avoidance and despair. Reshaping the self is not a pretty or an easy business.

The French expression *reculer pour mieux sauter* – to step back so you can jump better – applies to Nietzsche. Sometimes you can't just charge your way through tough times, Beckett or no Beckett. Sometimes you just have to *reculer*, that is, pull back into a zone of anxious, watchful avoidance – maybe even depression.

Self-awareness can be very painful, and many people spend their lives trying to fend it off in many different ways, through overwork, heavy drinking, drugs, compulsive sexual activity, even overtraining in the gym. So we *have to*, from time to time, *pull back*, that is, step out of the eager forward march-step of the approach system.

If we don't do that, then eventually we will hit a barrier that a flabby self, unused to reappraisal and untoughened by adjusting to adversity, will find so very hard to deal with. Joe faced that reality far too early in his life and he paid the price.

But I could think of many others of my old patients who had done the opposite – bulldozed on through life in a blind flight from self-awareness. Many were alcoholics, or on their way to becoming so. I remember one young man – Owen – who came to see me. His doctor had referred him because he was concerned he was drinking too much. He owned several bars and worked long hours building a very successful business.

'I aim to be a millionaire before I am thirty – and I'm going to do it!' Owen boasted. But he was drinking a lot and he couldn't sustain any long-term relationships with women. His doctor had detected that he was overdrinking in his liver function tests. But he was in full approach mode, with this burning goal to become a millionaire before he was thirty. He was nearly there and I could tell that the prospect of reaching it was bubbling away at the back of his mind. I could also see that it was making him anxious and that his drinking was partly a response to that anxiety.

What happens next? I knew he was being troubled by this thought, but he couldn't switch out of approach mode. Since the age of sixteen Owen had worked single-mindedly towards the aim of being a millionaire before he was thirty and now he was almost there. The problem was this, I only now realize with the benefit of hindsight: *he had become his goal*. His self was perched on this narrow stool and had never grown or developed because of his headlong, sixteen-hours-a-day quest to achieve a single goal.

I realized that he was like the Illinois lottery winners who ended up no happier than the people who had been paralysed in accidents. In fact, I suspect that he might have ended up very much unhappier than my brain- and spinal-injured patients because Owen's self had such a narrow foothold on life and he was likely to keep drinking more and more alcohol to stave off awareness of that fact.

Something told me, however, that there had to be more to this 'pulling back' than just self-awareness. Here was the problem: suppose Owen had cut down his drinking, toned down his approach mode and 'pulled back' into a reflective self-awareness. *What would he do then?* He had no idea. The prospect must have been terrifying for him. No wonder he drank so much.

There has to be more to finding balance than just self-reappraisal, I thought, and then it came to me: if I lose my legs, my looks, my job, my status or my life goal, I have to find some new basis for my self-esteem. What do I need in order to be able to do that? *Creativity.* To become stronger through what doesn't kill me, I must *create* new types of goals on which to base my self-evaluation. And that is no easy task.

So I turned back to the research yet again. When you pull back out of approach mode and into avoidance mode, does that make you more or less creative? This wasn't a random question because there is a lot of evidence to suggest that creative, 'divergent' thinking has a right hemisphere basis.[26] We know that avoidance mode is lateralized in the right hemisphere, so I wasn't completely wrong in predicting that avoidance mode might make me a little more creative – which, of course, is what is needed if I have to find new goals after a big setback.

There was evidence for this: people were asked to solve a type of puzzle called an 'insight problem'. This is one that can't be solved by logical, convergent thinking, but only by the looser, divergent thinking which is at the heart of creativity. Divergent thinking rests on weaker, less obvious links between ideas and concepts than convergent thinking. For example, try to find a single word that links these three: *tooth, heart, potato*. The answer here is not a strictly logical one, it is a rather 'lateral' one – *sweet*. Or consider these: *light, birthday, stick*, or try: *right, cat, carbon* (answers at the end of next paragraph).

In the test, before trying to solve these problems one group squeezed a rubber ball hard with their left hand for forty-five seconds four times, with a brief rest after each. Compared to a control group who didn't move their hands, they solved more of these creativity linked problems.[27] The explanation for this was that they activated the right half of their brains, just as happens in avoidance mode. Stimulating the right frontal lobe of the brain also boosts creativity, another study found.[28] (Answers to the three-word problems above: *candle* and *copy*.)

How could this be? The biggest obstacle to being creative is having to shake off previous assumptions, to *let go* your current perspective and *search broadly* for a different one. This is exactly what happens in the avoidance mode – you switch out of current goals, broaden your focus of attention and, often anxiously, scan the horizon for threat. But by doing this you also loosen up your mental framework and leave yourself open to new perceptions, new thoughts, new interpretations – and hence new opportunities.

So here was the other upside to pulling back that I had been looking for – the potential for imagining creative solutions to self-reassessment in the face of loss. Pulling back isn't necessarily bad, I realized; on the contrary, it offers the chance for re-imagining yourself in a way that is nearly impossible when you are locked into full success-oriented approach mode.

Gerry had used his period of mourning to re-imagine himself. Joe had not. He smoked cannabis to shy away from the self-awareness that is the tough midwife of a reappraised self. Also, he never seemed able – perhaps because the chronic cannabis use sapped his motivation – to switch out of avoidance and back into approach mode, which is essential to emotional resilience.

Harry Potter author J. K. Rowling talks in her 2008 Harvard commencement address about the benefits of failure.[29] As an impoverished, unemployed single parent she went through a dark period of life after the failure of a short-lived marriage. She felt she was in a darkened tunnel, with no idea whether there was any light at the end of it. But this withdrawal, this failure, had the effect of 'stripping away any of the inessential'. Had she succeeded at anything else, she might never have found the determination to be a writer, she says. Stripped of her previous goals she withdrew into a dark place from which a single, glittering goal emerged.

Harry Potter's creator really did seem to *reculer pour mieux sauter*. Not voluntarily, but forced by circumstance to withdraw from the old trappings of her self – of career, marriage and conventional success. In saying what she did she captured for me this strange mixture of approach and avoidance, reward and punishment, striving and withdrawal, satisfaction and anxiety, which I now believed was at the heart of how we should deal with adversity.

This zone of mental balance has a bitter-sweet character to it, I realized – just like life itself. It seems to me that you cannot achieve a Nietzschean strengthening without a degree of withdrawal, restraint and avoidance leading to often painful self-awareness and self-reappraisal. But neither is there any such strengthening without an equal amount of Beckett-inspired 'going on', an approach to life and to goals that may have no basis other than in an abstract hope and faith in the future.

Joe eventually did manage to 'go on' in his life again, but only after he stopped smoking cannabis and engaged with life and its setbacks. After some false starts, he went back to college to study photography and began to make a living from that. But it took a lot of self-appraisal and not a few avoidance-approach cycles before he found a balance zone around which to centre his new life. And that is what everyone has to do from time to time in their lives, for nothing stays the same and so nor can we stay the same.

What doesn't kill me *can* make me stronger, but only if I can use it to search out a balance of the self of the kind that so eluded my tormented friend Ken.

Epilogue

I pressed the start button on my computer and the machine whirred into life. Then my heart sank at the terse message that flashed up: 'Preparing Automatic Repair'. Suddenly anxious about the deadline I had to meet, I crossed my fingers and waited. The screen went black. Oh no! Then another message: 'Diagnosing your PC'. Phew, maybe it will fix itself. The screen blackened again, then the same message, then it went black again, then the same message, the screen blackened . . . on and on until I had to sprint to another office and borrow someone else's computer to finish the report.

My computer's software, I later found out, was caught in an 'infinite loop'. The reason for this, the technician told me, was that the software 'believed' that a particular event in the program would occur. That event was to have been the trigger for the software to end the current loop and go on to its next step. This would have been followed by the launch of the word processor that in turn would have let me write my overdue report. But the event never happened, so the program restarted the loop in the expectation of finding the key event the next time . . . and so on. The technician reinstalled the operating system and my computer worked fine again . . . for the time being at least.

Strangely enough, this recent experience jarred me out of my complacent assumption that I had solved the Nietzsche question as to why stress makes some people and breaks others. It did this by startling me into noticing a big, and very human, gap in my explanation so far.

That gap was *belief*.

Nietzsche was a vast figure with a big idea – that people can control their own destiny by exercising their 'will to power'. But the giant shadow he cast obscured a fundamental assumption behind this philosophy, which is that you can only exercise such power *if you believe that you have it*.

As this idea came upon me, suddenly one fact about my old patients struck me like a rock – almost all of them believed that their emotional difficulty was something external to themselves, something that 'came on' like an object or force out of the blue.

It felt to them, I surmised, like a freezing snowfall or a sudden storm. Perhaps, on reflection, 'fever' might be a better metaphor for how I think many of them experienced their anxieties, moods and depressions – particularly those whose doctors had prescribed pharmaceuticals or other physical treatments for their emotional problems.

My friend Ken, in whose car I had nearly met my end in Scotland, was an example of someone who had every right to feel that his highs and lows were like fevers sweeping over him out of his control. His severe bipolar disorder seemed clearly to be caused by some biochemical imbalance, albeit one that he could potentially have gained *some* control over, with the help of his medication. He showed early signs of 'going high' or 'going low' that, if detected early enough, he could sometimes nip in the bud, with the help of his family and doctors. But it was a constant struggle for him to keep within his own emotional balance zone and those unknown biochemical forces in his brain made this very, very difficult to do.

But many, maybe even most, of my other patients who didn't suffer from the sort of mental illness that Ken had also seemed to experience their emotional problems as fevers that were out of their control. Simon with the public-speaking phobia, for instance, believed this firmly and now, with the benefit of hindsight, I suddenly understood that this faulty belief was the single biggest obstacle to his recovery.

It was a barrier for two reasons. First, if you feel that your emotional problems are somehow external to you, then you can become scared of them. Simon told me that he had a sinking feeling in his stomach and a sense of dread when he felt a panic attack 'coming on'. This, of course, made the anxiety ramp up which made this 'thing' even more frightening, and so on in a dizzying upward spiral of anxiety. Fear of fear was the essential fuel for this emotional fire. Something similar can happen with depression – people who feel a depressed mood 'coming on' can have a sense of hopelessness and dread, which makes the mood worse. Feeling depressed about the depression is the fuel for the vicious cycle in this case.

The second reason why this belief in the 'thingness' of emotional problems is a barrier to recovery is simple: if they seem like a fever that you can't control, then you will feel that you simply have to sit it out and there is no point in trying to do something about it. So you won't take any of the steps that might otherwise keep you in an emotional balance.

For Nietzsche's maxim to apply, then, you *must* believe that you have some control over your emotions. Without this sense of at least potential control, then you won't be able to take the steps to make it more likely that what doesn't kill you, strengthens you.

Take Lucy, for instance, the student who reacted badly to a failed exam at the beginning of the book. As with Simon, it took me much longer to get her back on an even keel than it should have, because she felt her anxiety as a sort of fever that came over her. Her lack of a sense of control over this external emotional 'thing' was actually a major cause of that 'thing', I suddenly understood.

Her fellow student Peter was also stressed by what happened to him, but he took steps to do something about it. Why? Because he didn't see his emotional problems as fixed, but rather as dynamic processes brought on by the stressful events that were happening to him.

Lucy, however, felt paralysed by her anxiety as something fixed and controlled by forces outside of herself. And so she didn't do what Peter did and take steps to sort out the problems. She became frightened of her own fear and, as was the case for Simon, this lack of belief in her ability to control the 'thing' was actually one of the main reasons that turned her into an ashen-faced near-loner for several months.

The notion that what people *believe* contributes to their emotional problems has been simmering at the back of my mind for more than three decades. But only as I neared the end of writing this book did I put this together with a stream of research by a brilliant psychologist at Stanford University called Carol Dweck.

My computer had stuck in an infinite loop because it had the 'belief' that a particular event was going to happen. And though it never took place, this faulty belief locked the computer in an endless, fruitless cycle of trying the same pattern over and over again.

Carol Dweck discovered that early in life, children develop beliefs – theories – about themselves and who they are, for example, about their intelligence. There are two main types of theory that people have: *fixed* ('entity', in Dweck's terms) versus *malleable* ('incremental').[1] If you have a fixed theory of your intelligence, for example, you see it as something you are born with and so can't do much to change. But if you see your IQ as malleable, then you believe that it can be affected by what you do and what happens to you.

If you tend to agree with statements like *People have a more or less fixed quota of intelligence and can't change it much* and *No matter how much you learn, you can't really change your intelligence*, then you have a fixed theory of IQ. And you will disagree with statements like: *People can work to improve their intelligence* and *No matter how intelligent you already are, you can always improve it.* If you have a malleable theory of your IQ, you will disagree with the first two questions, and agree with the latter two.

Children and adults with fixed theories of their IQ, especially if they have been told by parents and teachers that they are 'bright', tend to react badly to failure in school, college or work where their intellectual abilities are being tested. This is because failure isn't something they think they can do anything about – for instance, working harder or taking another course. In their view, they were born 'bright' and there's nothing they can do about that except demonstrate how clever they are. If they fail in an exam or project at work, then, far from being a spur to work harder or learn more, it becomes a huge *threat* to their ego. 'Oh no, maybe I'm not so bright after all!'

This freezes up their thinking and means they don't learn from their failure: adolescents with fixed theories of their maths abilities, for instance, show a much smaller gain in maths performance over a year in school than those who hold malleable theories, irrespective of how good at maths they were at the start of the year.[2]

But here is the startling finding from Dweck's work that crystallized my long-held inkling about my patients' beliefs: people also have theories about their personalities that can be either fixed or malleable.[3]

Take the tough world of being a newbie in the schoolyard. Finding your group inevitably involves being rejected some of the time in this trial and error process. It turns out that children who have fixed theories about their personality, however, react badly to this rejection just as fixed-IQ people respond badly to failure.

Children with fixed personality theories are much more likely to withdraw into themselves and avoid trying again because they tend to see the reason for the rejection as something *inside* them: that is, 'I'm no good at getting on with other kids' (a fixed theory) rather than 'They're a real clique – I should try someone else' (a malleable theory). They can stop making efforts to make new friends because they think there is something wrong with their own personality. And so they can end up becoming unpopular because they *avoid* doing the things that could make them accepted – all because they are handicapped by a helplessness-inducing fatalism about the fixed nature of their personality.

It applies to eating and weight problems also. People who have the fixed theory that they are genetically programmed to be fat tend to eat much more unhealthily, not take exercise, and as a consequence have worse physical health than do people who believe that what they do as well as what genes they have play a part in their weight.[4] In almost all of my patients I have found myself grappling with what seemed to be the biggest challenge for them – a feeling of *helplessness* in the face of their emotional problems. Only now am I beginning to understand that their beliefs about what caused their anxiety, anger or depression is almost certainly a major reason for this sense of out-of-control fatalism. In fact, I begin to wonder whether this belief *was* the core problem for some of them.

Peter, the student I discussed in the prologue, had been very stressed by the death of his mother and his subsequent difficulties but he hadn't sought help himself – his tutor had referred him to me because he was concerned about him. But Peter hadn't needed much help from me and it struck me that this was because he didn't have a fixed theory of his emotions and personality: rather, he saw his anxiety and stress as a response to a difficult situation and used this to energize him into what ended up as being a very positive result for both him and his family.

Lucy, on the other hand, seemed to me in retrospect to have had a fixed theory about her emotions and personality. And she reacted badly to a minor academic failure for two reasons. One is that she also had a fixed view of her IQ, and this failure was therefore a blow to her self-image as a clever student. Another was that once the anxiety came on – something she had never in her blessed life experienced before – she applied her fixed theory to this as well. And so she saw the cause of her emotional difficulty as a flaw in herself, rather than as a malleable response to a changeable situation.

Carol Dweck showed exactly this Peter–Lucy difference in a study of low mood among college students. When a student shown by their questionnaire responses to have a fixed theory of their personality later had a spell of feeling depressed, it reduced their efforts and ability to cope, exactly as had happened to Lucy.

But when a student with a malleable theory of their personality had a spell of low mood, it *boosted* their ability and efforts to cope by *energizing them*.[5] This was precisely what happened to Peter.

And there was more evidence for this, I discovered: young adolescents who 'attributed' bad experiences to causes *inside* themselves – they had fixed theories, in other words – were much more likely to become depressed over a five-year period than those who had malleable, dynamic theories about stress.[6]

Lucy was at a high risk of becoming even more depressed than she already was, I am pretty sure, if I hadn't seen her. In the 1970s, though, it is unlikely that she would have been prescribed antidepressants. But in the twenty-first century she almost certainly would have been – remember the fifty-three million prescriptions for fifty-three million English citizens in 2013.

And suddenly all the memories came back – wheeling the trolleys for Monday morning 'treatment' in New Zealand, debates with psychiatry colleagues at the Maudsley Hospital and my own dogmatic 'the brain is not a muscle' lectures in Edinburgh. All at once I realized that the hardware–software debate was not one of just academic interest: yes, we have to consider both, and finding the balance means that you must accept that mental software can reshape the brain hardware and vice versa.

But the crucial issue about hardware and software, I have come to understand, is what you *believe*. If Lucy's doctor had prescribed her antidepressants, what effect would they have had on her theory about herself? She was being given the message that there was something wrong with the hardware of her brain, thereby reinforcing her fixed theory of her emotional state.

But there was nothing wrong with the hardware of Lucy's brain. So would my task of helping her reprogram her mental software have been even harder had she bought into the hardware–fault, fixed theory of her emotions by taking antidepressants?

I have big worries about the epidemic of prescriptions for depression and anxiety. Could one side effect of all this be that it reduces people's ability to cope by building fixed rather than malleable theories in their minds? If that is true, then it means that our ability to use stress to make us stronger is being undermined by a culture that medicalizes our emotional problems, making 'things' out of them and so creating a sense of helplessness in the face of them. I fear that there will be many more Lucys and many fewer Peters in the coming years than there ever were in the 1970s.

Of course we need good antidepressants and other drugs for the hardware faults of the brain; for example, my friend Ken would never have survived as long as he did without the excellent pharmaceuticals that my colleagues at the Institute of Psychiatry have helped develop. And I did see profoundly depressed patients respond remarkably to hardware-focused drug and ECT treatments.

I am not drifting into an anti-psychiatry position after all these years, but I *am* very worried about the epidemic of prescriptions of drugs for hundreds of millions of people worldwide, many of whose problems are no more severe than Lucy's or Peter's. But what really concerns me is what Fiona O'Doherty has warned me about for the last decade – that the biggest negative side effect of all this could be the fostering of fixed theories of emotion that in turn diminish people's ability to use Nietzsche's maxim to benefit from stress in the way that Peter had. Fixed theories make people more depressed by undercutting their belief in their ability to control their emotions.

Gloria, paralysed by a deep-seated anxiety, had been prescribed both anti-anxiety and antidepressant drugs, and, given her lifelong anxiety, I doubt that being prescribed these would have had much effect on her belief that her emotional problems were beyond her control. But, nevertheless, she did have a fixed theory of her problems, and this made her very pessimistic about taking any practical steps towards facing up to them. If she had come to see me today I think I would have tried to tackle her pessimistic beliefs about not having control before attempting to shift her out of her chronic avoidance and into a more approach mode.

Joe was another casualty of the beliefs he had about himself. He was caught in an infinite loop of trying to reconcile the way his life had gone with the fixed theory he held of himself as a bright, gifted, golden boy to whom success came without effort. 'Without effort' is the key here – Joe's parents had always praised him for being 'bright' and so had built a strong fixed theory of IQ in his mind. When he unprecedentedly failed an exam, that was not a mere failure, it was in his mind a dreadful sign that maybe he was wrong about being clever – and it was such a threat to his ego that he spent years running away from it.

Something similar applied to Joe's personality – he had never known what it was like to be rejected or to have to work at being accepted by others. His glowing personality was a 'thing', a fixed entity with which he had been blessed and he had no conception of the fact that most people have to work at becoming who they are by trial and error, by sometimes painfully rethinking themselves and, most of all, by the sheer grit of 'going on'.

When his parents split up and then his girlfriend broke off their relationship, Joe's fixed theory of his personality as something he was born with meant that he didn't believe that he could do anything to change his situation. Instead, he had to battle with a massive threat to his ego – 'maybe I'm not the golden boy loved by everyone' – and with the impossible task of reconciling the facts on the ground with his theory of himself. Joe could only dull the ache of this endless discordance between theory and reality with cannabis. His strange, somewhat haughty passivity that had so perplexed me when I first met him now made sense – he was caught in an infinite loop as he tried to close the unbridgeable gap between the theory and the reality of his life.

If only I had realized earlier that my patients' theories about their emotional problems – and hence about whether they had any control over them – were key to how they coped with stress. If their personalities were fixed 'things' that they had inherited, then so were their emotional disorders. So how could they possibly summon the determination to persist through anxiety-arousing setbacks and struggle while learning to control them? After all, weren't they uncontrollable, according to their theories?

Whenever I suggested goals as part of cognitive behaviour therapy to these patients, I sometimes felt a sort of 'resistance' from them that I had never quite managed to put my finger on. Doubtless there were some unconscious processes at work some of the time that a psychotherapist with a different approach from mine could identify better than I could. But I have now become convinced that a big part of that 'resistance' was, in fact, the patients' fatalistic lack of belief in the possibility of control over their own minds, which stemmed from their fixed theories of their emotional problems.

If what doesn't kill you *is* to strengthen you, then you have to *believe* that you have some control over your own mind and emotions. Without that conviction, you will not be able to put in place the other ingredients of resilience that I have identified in the course of this book. With that belief, every single human being has the capacity of using what we know about the way the software and hardware of our brains interact to keep, wherever possible, nearer to a balance between mental extremes – between being fatigued and stressed out, chilled out and alert, between approaching and avoiding, self-forgetting and self-awareness, among many others.

Above all, we have to believe that many of the symptoms of stress are also symptoms of excitement, and of anger. Low mood shares symptoms with extreme tiredness and low arousal. We have the ability to gain some control over these emotions by the way we label them in our minds. But we have to believe in their *malleability*, and not cripple ourselves by false theories that these and our personalities are fixed. I hope that this book will help readers understand their own beliefs and so become more confident about being able to shape their own mental abilities, motivation and emotional balance by understanding better what determines these states.

For only by believing that we have some such control can we use the magnificent malleable complexity of the brain, and the mental software that controls it, to find the right mental balance we need for each challenge that faces us.

Notes

Prologue

1. Chapman, A. and M. Chapman-Santana (1995), 'The influence of Nietzsche on Freud's ideas'. *British Journal of Psychiatry*, 166(2), 251–3.
2. Nietzsche, F. W. (2001), *Twilight of the Idols with the Antichrist and Ecce Homo*. London: Wordsworth Editions.
3. Batstone, W. (1996), 'The fragments of Furius Antias'. *Classical Quarterly* (New Series), 46(02), 387–402.
4. HSCIC (2013) a.I. *Statins, antidepressants, diabetes prescribing items and NIC 1991 to 2013* [cited 27 April 2015]; Available from: http://www.hscic. gov.uk/article/2021/Website-Search?q=anti-depressants&go=Go&area=both.
5. Merzenich, M. M., et al. (1983), 'Progression of change following median nerve section in the cortical representation of the hand in areas 3b and 1 in adult owl and squirrel monkeys'. *Neuroscience*, 10(3), 639–65.
6. Jenkins, W. M., M. M. Merzenich and G. Recanzone (1990), 'Neocortical representational dynamics in adult primates: implications for neuropsychology'. *Neuropsychologia*, 28(6), 573–84.
7. Rossini, P., et al. (1994), 'Short-term brain "plasticity" in humans: transient finger representation changes in sensory cortex somatotopy following ischemic anesthesia'. *Brain Research*, 642(1), 169–77.
8. Sadato, N., et al. (1996), 'Activation of the primary visual cortex by Braille reading in blind subjects'. *Nature*, 380, 526–8.
9. Clark, S. A., et al. (1988), 'Receptive fields in the body-surface map in adult cortex defined by temporally correlated inputs'. *Nature*, 332, 444–5.
10. Recanzone, G. H., C. E. Schreiner and M. M. Merzenich (1993), 'Plasticity in the frequency representation of primary auditory cortex'. *Journal of Neuroscience*, 13, 87–103.

11. Tallal, P., et al. (1996), 'Language comprehension in language-learning impaired children improved with acoustically modified speech'. *Science*, 271, 81–4.

12. Mishra, J., et al. (2014), 'Adaptive training diminishes distractibility in aging across species'. *Neuron*, 84(5), 1091–1103.

13. Maguire, E. A., et al. (2000), 'Navigation-related structural change in the hippocampi of taxi drivers'. *Proceedings of the National Academy of Sciences, USA*, 97, 4398–4403.

14. Moutsiana, C., et al. (2015), 'Insecure attachment during infancy predicts greater amygdala volumes in early adulthood'. *Journal of Child Psychology and Psychiatry*, 56(5), 540–8.

15. Glaser, R., et al. (1990), 'Psychological Stress-Induced Modulation of Interleukin 2 Receptor Gene Expression and Interleukin 2 Production in Peripheral Blood Leukocytes'. *Archives of General Psychiatry*, 47(8), 707–12.

16. Sotnikov, S. V., et al. (2014), 'Bidirectional rescue of extreme genetic predispositions to anxiety: impact of CRH receptor 1 as epigenetic plasticity gene in the amygdala'. *Translational Psychiatry*, 4, e359.

17. Fares, R. P., et al. (2013), 'Standardized environmental enrichment supports enhanced brain plasticity in healthy rats and prevents cognitive impairment in epileptic rats'. *PLOS ONE*, 8(1), e53888.

18. Lopez-Maury, L., S. Marguerat and J. Bahler (2008), 'Tuning gene expression to changing environments: from rapid responses to evolutionary adaptation'. *Nature Reviews Genetics*, 9(8), 583–93.

19. Glaser et al., 'Psychological Stress'.

20. Brydon, L., et al. (2005), 'Psychological stress activates interleukin-1β gene expression in human mononuclear cells'. *Brain, Behavior, and Immunity*, 19(6), 540–6.

21. Saxena, S., et al. (2009), 'Rapid effects of brief intensive cognitive-behavioral therapy on brain glucose metabolism in obsessive-compulsive disorder'. *Molecular Psychiatry*, 14(2), 197–205.

22. McNab, F., et al. (2009), 'Changes in Cortical Dopamine D1 Receptor Binding Associated with Cognitive Training'. *Science*, 323(5915), 800–2.

23. Robertson, I. (1999), *Mind Sculpture*. London: Bantam.

1: Why Do Engineers Build Bends in Roads?

1. Robertson, I. H., et al. (1997), '"Oops!": performance correlates of everyday attentional failures in traumatic brain injured and normal subjects'. *Neuropsychologia*, 35, 747–58.

2. Manly, T., et al. (2003), 'Enhancing the sensitivity of a sustained attention task to frontal damage. Convergent clinical and functional imaging evidence'. *Neurocase*, 9, 340–9.

3. Edkins, G. and C. Pollock (1997), 'The influence of sustained attention on railway accidents'. *Accident Analysis and Prevention*, 29, 533–9.

4. Manly, T., et al. (2002), 'Coffee in the cornflakes: Time-of-day as a modulator of executive response control'. *Neuropsychologia*, 40, 1–6.

5. Aston-Jones, G., et al. (2001), 'A neural circuit for circadian regulation of arousal and performance'. *Nature Neuroscience*, 4, 732–8.

6. Sara, S. J. (2009), 'The locus coeruleus and noradrenergic modulation of cognition'. *Nature Reviews Neuroscience*, 10, 211–23.

7. Saper, C. B., T. E. Scammell and J. Lu (2005), 'Hypothalamic regulation of sleep and circadian rhythms'. *Nature*, 437(7063), 1257–63.

8. Bellgrove, M. A., et al. (2006), 'The Cognitive Genetics of Attention Deficit Hyperactivity Disorder (ADHD): Sustained attention as a Candidate Phenotype'. *Cortex*, 42, 838–45.

9. Greene, C., et al. (2009), 'Noradrenergic genotype predicts lapses in sustained attention'. *Neuropsychologia*, 47, 591–4.

10. Manly, T., et al. (1999), 'The absent mind: Further investigations of sustained attention to response'. *Neuropsychologia*, 37, 661–70.

11. Smilek, D., J. S. A. Carriere and J. A. Cheyne (2010), 'Failures of sustained attention in life, lab, and brain: Ecological validity of the SART'. *Neuropsychologia*, 48(9), 2564–70.

12. Manly et al., 'The absent mind'.

13. Manly, T., et al. (in press), 'Enhancing the sensitivity of a sustained attention task to frontal damage. Convergent clinical and functional imaging evidence'. *Neurocase*.

14. O'Connor, C., I. H. Robertson and B. Levine (2011), 'The prosthetics of vigilant attention: random cuing cuts processing demands'. *Neuropsychology*, 25(4), 535–43.

15. Robertson, I. H., et al. (1998), 'Phasic alerting of neglect patients overcomes their spatial deficit in visual awareness'. *Nature*, 395(10), 169–72.

16. Manly, T., et al. (2002), 'Rehabilitation of Executive Function: Facilitation of effective goal management on complex tasks using periodic auditory alerts'. *Neuropsychologia*, 40, 271–81.

17. Robertson, I. H., et al. (1995), 'Sustained attention training for unilateral neglect: theoretical and rehabilitation implications'. *Journal of Clinical and Experimental Neuropsychology*, 17, 416–30.

18. Murphy, P., et al. (2014), 'Pupil Diameter Covaries with BOLD Activity in Human Locus Coeruleus'. *Human Brain Mapping*, 35, 4140–54.

19. Yamamoto, K.-i., H. Arai and S. Nakayama (1990), 'Skin conductance response after 6-hydroxydopamine lesion of central noradrenaline system in cats'. *Biological Psychiatry*, 28(2), 151–60.

20. Storm, H., et al. (2002), 'Skin conductance correlates with perioperative stress'. *Acta Anaesthesiologica Scandinavica*, 46(7), 887–95.
21. Bradley, M. M., et al. (2008), 'The pupil as a measure of emotional arousal and autonomic activation'. *Psychophysiology*, 45(4), 602–7.
22. O'Connell, R. G., et al. (2008), 'Self-Alert Training: Volitional modulation of autonomic arousal improves sustained attention'. *Neuropsychologia*, 46(5), 1379–90.
23. Salomone, S., et al. (2012), 'A biofeedback-based programme to improve attention and impulsivity in adults with ADHD'. *Irish Journal of Psychology*, 33, 86–93.

2: *What a New Zealand Earthquake Taught Me About Nietzsche*

1. Helton, W. and J. Head (2012), 'Earthquakes on the Mind: Implications of Disasters for Human Performance'. *Human Factors*, 54, 189–94.
2. Yerkes, R. M. and J. D. Dodson (1908), 'The relation of strength of stimulus to rapidity of habit-formation'. *Journal of Comparative and Neurological Psychology*, 18, 459–82.
3. Beilock, S. L. (2008), 'Math performance in stressful situations'. *Current Directions in Psychological Science*, 17(5), 339–43.
4. Killingsworth, M. A. and D. T. Gilbert (2010), 'A Wandering Mind Is an Unhappy Mind'. *Science*, 330(6006), 932.
5. McVay, J. C., M. J. Kane and T. R. Kwapil (2009), 'Tracking the train of thought from the laboratory into everyday life: An experience-sampling study of mind wandering across controlled and ecological contexts'. *Psychonomic Bulletin & Review*, 16(5), 857–63.
6. Buckner, R. L. and D. C. Carroll (2007), 'Self-projection and the brain'. *Trends in Cognitive Sciences*, 11(2), 49–57.
7. Somerville, L. H., et al. (2013), 'The Medial Prefrontal Cortex and the Emergence of Self-Conscious Emotion in Adolescence'. *Psychological Science*, 24(8), 1554–62.

3: *Rodin and the Goalkeeper*

1. Morrow, L., et al. (1981), 'Arousal responses to emotional stimuli and laterality of lesion'. *Neuropsychologia*, 19, 65–71.

2. Heilman, K. M., H. D. Schwartz and R. T. Watson (1978), 'Hypoarousal in patients with the neglect syndrome and emotional indifference'. *Neurology*, 28, 229–32.

3. Güntürkün, O. (2003), 'Human behaviour: Adult persistence of head-turning asymmetry'. *Nature*, 421, 711.

4. Joanette, Y., et al. (1986), 'Pointing with left vs right hand in left visual field neglect'. *Neuropsychologia*, 24(3), 391–6.

5. Robertson, I. H. and N. North (1992), 'Spatio-motor cueing in unilateral neglect: The role of hemispace, hand and motor activation'. *Neuropsychologia*, 30, 553–63.

6. Robertson, I. H. and N. North (1993), 'Active and passive activation of left limbs: influence on visual and sensory neglect'. *Neuropsychologia*, 31, 293–300.

7. Robertson, I. H. and N. North (1994), 'One hand is better than two: Motor extinction of left hand advantage in unilateral neglect'. *Neuropsychologia*, 32, 1–11.

8. Roskes, M., et al. (2011), 'The Right Side? Under Time Pressure, Approach Motivation Leads to Right-Oriented Bias'. *Psychological Science*, 22(11), 1403–7.

9. Quaranta, A., M. Siniscalchi and G. Vallortigara (2007), 'Asymmetric tail-wagging responses by dogs to different emotive stimuli'. *Current Biology*, 17(6), R199–201.

10. Beckett, S. (1960), *The Unnamable*. London: Calder and Boyers.

11. Beckett, S. (1983), *Worstward Ho*. London: Calder.

12. Robertson, I. H., et al. (2002), 'Rehabilitation by Limb Activation Training (LAT) Reduces Impairment in Unilateral Neglect Patients: A Single-Blind Randomised Control Trial'. *Neuropsychological Rehabilitation*, 12, 439–54.

13. Robertson, I. (2012), *The Winner Effect: How Power Affects Your Brain*. London: Bloomsbury.

14. Wilkinson, D., et al. (2010), 'Feeling socially powerless makes you more prone to bumping into things on the right and induces leftward line bisection error'. *Psychonomic Bulletin & Review*, 17(6), 910–14.

15. Boksem, M. A. S., R. Smolders and D. D. Cremer (2012), 'Social power and approach-related neural activity'. *Social Cognitive and Affective Neuroscience*, 7(5), 516–20.

16. Garavan, H., T. J. Ross and E. A. Stein (1999), 'Right hemispheric dominance of inhibitory control: an event-related fMRI study'. *Proceedings of the National Academy of Sciences, USA*, 96, 8301–6.

17. Gray, J. A. (1990), 'Brain systems that mediate both emotion and cognition'. *Cognition & Emotion*, 4(3), 269–88.

18. Davidson, R. J. (1992), 'Anterior cerebral asymmetry and the nature of emotion'. *Brain and Cognition*, 20(1), 125–51.

19. Toga, A. and P. Thompson (2003), 'Mapping Brain Asymmetry'. *Nature Reviews Neuroscience*, 4, 37–48.
20. Montani, V., M. De Filippo De Grazia and M. Zorzi (2014), 'A new adaptive videogame for training attention and executive functions: Design principles and initial validation'. *Frontiers in Psychology*, 13,5, 409.
21. Oke, A., et al. (1978), 'Lateralization of norepinephrine in human thalamus'. *Science*, 200: 1411–13.
22. Davidson, 'Anterior cerebral asymmetry'.
23. Tomer, R., et al. (2008), 'Incentive motivation is associated with striatal dopamine asymmetry'. *Biological Psychology*, 77(1), 98–101.
24. Wacker, J., et al. (2013), 'Dopamine-D2-receptor blockade reverses the association between trait approach motivation and frontal asymmetry in an approach-motivation context'. *Psychological Science*, 24(4), 489–97.
25. McGregor, I., K. A. Nash and M. Inzlicht (2009), 'Threat, high self-esteem, and reactive approach-motivation: Electroencephalographic evidence'. *Journal of Experimental Social Psychology*, 45(4), 1003–7.
26. Niedenthal, P. M. (2007), 'Embodying Emotion'. *Science*, 316(5827), 1002–5.
27. Ibid.
28. Davidson, 'Anterior cerebral asymmetry'.
29. Davidson, R. J. and N. A. Fox (1989), 'Frontal brain asymmetry predicts infants' response to maternal separation'. *Journal of Abnormal Psychology*, 98(2), 127.
30. Buss, K. A., et al. (2003), 'Right frontal brain activity, cortisol, and withdrawal behavior in 6-month-old infants'. *Behavioral Neuroscience*, 117, 11–20.
31. Shackman, A. J., et al. (2009), 'Right Dorsolateral Prefrontal Cortical Activity and Behavioral Inhibition'. *Psychological Science*, 20(12), 1500–6.
32. Harmon-Jones, E. (2006), 'Unilateral right-hand contractions cause contralateral alpha power suppression and approach motivational affective experience'. *Psychophysiology*, 43(6), 598–603.
33. Schiff, B. B. and M. Lamon (1994), 'Inducing emotion by unilateral contraction of hand muscles'. *Cortex*, 30(2), 247–54.
34. Carney, D. R., A. J. C. Cuddy and A. J. Yap (2010), 'Power Posing'. *Psychological Science*, 21(10), 1363–8.
35. McGregor, Nash and Inzlicht, 'Threat, high self-esteem, and reactive approach-motivation'.

4: Sex and the Suspension Bridge

1. Dutton, D. G. and A. P. Aron (1974), 'Some evidence for heightened sexual attraction under conditions of high anxiety'. *Journal of Personality and Social Psychology*, 30(4), 510.

2. Reisenzein, R. (1983), 'The Schachter theory of emotion: two decades later'. *Psychological Bulletin*, 94(2), 239.

3. Meston, C. M. and P. F. Frohlich (2003), 'Love at first fright: Partner salience moderates roller-coaster-induced excitation transfer'. *Archives of Sexual Behavior*, 32(6), 537–44.

4. Rivier, C. and S. Rivest (1991), 'Effect of stress on the activity of the hypothalamic-pituitary-gonadal axis: peripheral and central mechanisms'. *Biology of Reproduction*, 45(4), 523–32.

5. Nepomnaschy, P. A., et al. (2006), 'Cortisol levels and very early pregnancy loss in humans'. *Proceedings of the National Academy of Sciences, USA*, 103(10), 3938–42.

6. Schachter, S. and J. Singer (1962), 'Cognitive, social, and physiological determinants of emotional state'. *Psychological Review*, 69(5), 379.

7. White, G. L., S. Fishbein and J. Rutsein (1981), 'Passionate love and the misattribution of arousal'. *Journal of Personality and Social Psychology*, 41(1), 56.

8. Brooks, A. W. (2014), 'Get excited: Reappraising pre-performance anxiety as excitement'. *Journal of Experimental Psychology: General*, 143(3), 1144.

9. Johnson, A., *Dallaire opens up about four suicide attempts*. CTV News, 19 May 2012 [cited 2 May 2015]; Available from: http://www.ctvnews.ca/dallaire-opens-up-about-four-suicide-attempts-1.707796.

10. *UN general's Rwandan nightmares*. BBC News, 5 July 2000 [cited 2 May 2015]; Available from: http://news.bbc.co.uk/2/hi/africa/820827.stm.

11. Harmon-Jones, E. (2003), 'Anger and the behavioral approach system'. *Personality and Individual Differences*, 35(5), 995–1005.

12. Carver, C. S. and E. Harmon-Jones (2009), 'Anger is an approach-related affect: evidence and implications'. *Psychological Bulletin*, 135(2), 183.

13. Orth, U. and E. Wieland (2006), 'Anger, hostility, and posttraumatic stress disorder in trauma-exposed adults: A meta-analysis'. *Journal of Consulting and Clinical Psychology*, 74(4), 698.

14. Carver and Harmon-Jones, 'Anger is an approach-related affect'.

15. Ibid.

16. Orth and Wieland, 'Anger, hostility and posttraumatic stress disorder'.

17. Kelley, N. J., R. Hortensius and E. Harmon-Jones (2013), 'When Anger Leads to Rumination: Induction of Relative Right Frontal Cortical Activity With Transcranial Direct Current Stimulation Increases Anger-Related Rumination'. *Psychological Science*, 24(4) 475–81.

18. Ibid.

19. Tamir, M., C. Mitchell and J. J. Gross (2008), 'Hedonic and instrumental motives in anger regulation'. *Psychological Science*, 19(4), 324–8.

20. Sell, A., J. Tooby and L. Cosmides (2009), 'Formidability and the logic of human anger'. *Proceedings of the National Academy of Sciences, USA*, 106(35), 15073–8.

21. Wacker, J., et al. (2013), 'Dopamine-D2-receptor blockade reverses the association between trait approach motivation and frontal asymmetry in an approach-motivation context'. *Psychological Science*, 24(4), 489–97.
22. *CNN News*, 28 May 2014.
23. Lovett, I. 'Rampage Victims Drawn to California Campus From Near and From Far.' *New York Times*, 25 May 2014.
24. Inzlicht, M., L. Legault and R. Teper (2014), 'Exploring the Mechanisms of Self-Control Improvement'. *Current Directions in Psychological Science*, 23(4), 302–7.
25. Lerner, J. S., et al. (2007), 'Facial Expressions of Emotion Reveal Neuroendocrine and Cardiovascular Stress Responses'. *Biological Psychiatry*, 61(2), 253–60.
26. Lawson-Tancred, H. (1991), *Aristotle: The Art of Rhetoric*. London: Penguin Books.
27. Miller, T. Q., et al. (1996), 'Meta-analytic review of research on hostility and physical health'. *Psychological Bulletin*, 119(2), 322.
28. Davidson, K., et al. (2000), 'Constructive anger verbal behavior predicts blood pressure in a population-based sample'. *Health Psychology*, 19(1), 55.
29. Davidson, K., et al. (1999), 'Increasing constructive anger verbal behavior decreases resting blood pressure: a secondary analysis of a randomized controlled hostility intervention'. *International Journal of Behavioral Medicine*, 6(3), 268–78.
30. Ochsner, K. N., et al. (2002), 'Rethinking Feelings: An fMRI Study of the Cognitive Regulation of Emotion'. *Journal of Cognitive Neuroscience*, 14, 1215–29.
31. Goldin, P. R., et al. (2008), 'The Neural Bases of Emotion Regulation: Reappraisal and Suppression of Negative Emotion'. *Biological Psychiatry*, 63(6), 577–86.
32. Gross, J. J. (2002), 'Emotion regulation: Affective, cognitive, and social consequences'. *Psychophysiology*, 39(3), 281–91.
33. Ibid.

5: How Can Stress Make You Smarter?

1. Feeney, J., et al. (2013), 'Cognitive Function Is Preserved in Older Adults With a Reported History of Childhood Sexual Abuse'. *Journal of Traumatic Stress*, 26(6), 735–43.
2. Ritchie, K., et al. (2011), 'Adverse childhood environment and late-life cognitive functioning'. *International Journal of Geriatric Psychiatry*, 26(5), 503–10.

3. Comijs, H. C., et al. (2011), 'Accumulated and Differential Effects of Life Events on Cognitive Decline in Older Persons: Depending on Depression, Baseline Cognition, or ApoE ε4 Status?' *Journals of Gerontology Series B: Psychological Sciences and Social Sciences*, 66B(suppl 1), i111–i120.

4. Rosnick, C. B., et al. (2007), 'Negative Life Events and Cognitive Performance in a Population of Older Adults'. *Journal of Aging and Health*, 19(4), 612–29.

5. Plassman, B. L., et al. (2011), 'Incidence of dementia and cognitive impairment, not dementia in the United States'. *Annals of Neurology*, 70(3), 418–26.

6. Ott, A., et al. (1995), 'Prevalence of Alzheimer's disease and vascular dementia: association with education. The Rotterdam study'. *British Medical Journal*, 310(6985), 970–3.

7. Parker, E. S. and E. P. Noble (1977), 'Alcohol consumption and cognitive functioning in social drinkers'. *Journal of Studies on Alcohol and Drugs*, 38(07), 1224.

8. Robertson, I. (1984), 'Does moderate drinking cause mental impairment?' *British Medical Journal* (Clinical Research edn), 289(6447), 711.

9. Gatz, M., et al. (2007), 'Accounting for the relationship between low education and dementia: A twin study'. *Physiology & Behavior*, 92(1–2), 232–7.

10. Draganski, B., et al. (2006), 'Temporal and Spatial Dynamics of Brain Structure Changes during Extensive Learning'. *Journal of Neuroscience*, 26(23), 6314–17.

11. Ibid.

12. Maguire, E. A., et al (2000), 'Navigation-related structural change in the hippocampi of taxi drivers'. *Proceedings of The National Academy of Sciences*, 97, 4398–4403.

13. Draganski et al., 'Temporal and Spatial Dynamics of Brain Structure Changes'.

14. Valenzuela, M. J., et al. (2011), 'Multiple Biological Pathways Link Cognitive Lifestyle to Protection from Dementia'. *Biological Psychiatry*, 71, 783–91.

15. Bennett, D. A., et al. (2006), 'The effect of social networks on the relation between Alzheimer's disease pathology and level of cognitive function in old people: a longitudinal cohort study'. *Lancet Neurology*, 5(5), 406–12.

16. Verghese, J., et al. (2003), 'Leisure Activities and the Risk of Dementia in the Elderly'. *New England Journal of Medicine*, 348(25), 2508–16.

17. Klusmann, V., et al. (2010), 'Complex Mental and Physical Activity in Older Women and Cognitive Performance: A 6-month Randomized Controlled Trial'. *Journals of Gerontology Series A: Biological Sciences and Medical Sciences*, 65A(6), 680–8.

18. Valenzuela, M. and P. Sachdev (2009), 'Can Cognitive Exercise Prevent the Onset of Dementia? Systematic Review of Randomized Clinical Trials with Longitudinal Follow-up'. *American Journal of Geriatric Psychiatry*, 17(3), 179–87.

19. Rundek, T. and D. A. Bennett (2006), 'Cognitive leisure activities, but not watching TV, for future brain benefits'. *Neurology*, 66(6), 794–5.

20. Csikszentmihalyi, M. and R. Kubey (1981), 'Television and the Rest of Life: A Systematic Comparison of Subjective Experience'. *Public Opinion Quarterly*, 45(3), 317–28.

21. Depp, C. A., et al. (2010), 'Age, affective experience, and television use'. *American Journal of Preventive Medicine*, 39(2), 173–8.

22. Valenzuela, M. J. and P. Sachdev (2006), 'Brain reserve and dementia: a systematic review'. *Psychological Medicine*, 36(04), 441–54.

23. Baroncelli, L., et al. (2010), 'Nurturing brain plasticity: impact of environmental enrichment'. *Cell Death and Differentiation*, 17, 1092–1103.

24. Catlow, B. J., et al. (2009), 'Effects of environmental enrichment and physical activity on neurogenesis in transgenic PS1/APP mice'. *Brain Research*, 1256(0), 173–9.

25. Veyrac, A., et al. (2008), 'Novelty Determines the Effects of Olfactory Enrichment on Memory and Neurogenesis Through Noradrenergic Mechanisms'. *Neuropsychopharmacology*, 34, 786–95.

26. Robertson, I. H. (2014), 'A right hemisphere role in cognitive reserve'. *Neurobiology of Aging*, 35(6), 1375–85.

27. Naka, F., et al. (2002), 'An enriched environment increases noradrenaline concentration in the mouse brain'. *Brain Research*, 924(1), 124–6.

28. Feinstein, D. L., et al. (2002), 'Noradrenergic regulation of inflammatory gene expression in brain'. *Neurochemistry International*, 41(5), 357–65.

29. Heneka, M. T., et al. (2010), 'Locus coeruleus controls Alzheimer's disease pathology by modulating microglial functions through norepinephrine'. *Proceedings of the National Academy of Sciences, USA*, 107(13), 6058–63.

30. Robertson, I. H. (2013), 'A noradrenergic theory of cognitive reserve: implications for Alzheimer's disease'. *Neurobiology of Aging*, 34, 298–308.

31. Murphy, P., et al. (2014), 'Pupil Diameter Covaries with BOLD Activity in Human Locus Coeruleus'. *Human Brain Mapping*, 35, 4140–54.

32. Bornemann, B., et al. (2010), 'Mathematical cognition: individual differences in resource allocation'. *ZDM*, 42(6), 555–67.

33. Van Der Meer, E., et al. (2010), 'Resource allocation and fluid intelligence: Insights from pupillometry'. *Psychophysiology*, 47(1), 158–69.

34. Robertson (2013), 'A noradrenergic theory of cognitive reserve' *Neurobiology of Aging*, 34, 298–308.

35. Wilson, R. S., et al. (20130, 'Neural reserve, neuronal density in the locus coeruleus, and cognitive decline'. *Neurology*, 80, 1202–8.

36. Ibid.
37. Clewett, D.V., et al. (2015), 'Neuromelanin marks the spot: identifying a locus coeruleus biomarker of cognitive reserve in healthy aging'. *Neurobiology of Aging* 37, 117–126.
38 Rohwedder, S. and R. Willis (2010), 'Mental Retirement'. *Journal of Economic Perspectives*, 24, 119–38.
39. Dufouil, C., et al. (2013), 'Older age at retirement is associated with decreased risk of dementia: Analysis of a health care insurance database of self-employed workers'. *Alzheimer's & Dementia: The Journal of the Alzheimer's Association*, 9, 342–343.
40. Bremner, J. D., et al. (1995), 'MRI-based measurement of hippocampal volume in patients with combat-related posttraumatic-stress-disorder'. *American Journal of Psychiatry*, 152, 973–81.
41. Chen, L., et al. (2013), 'Impact of acute stress on human brain microstructure: An MR diffusion study of earthquake survivors'. *Human Brain Mapping*, 34(2), 367–73.
42. Wilson, R. S., et al. (2003), 'Proneness to psychological distress is associated with risk of Alzheimer's disease'. *Neurology*, 61(11), 1479–85.
43. Keenan, B. (1992), *An Evil Cradling*. London: Vintage.
44. Pruessner, J. C., et al. (2005), 'Self-esteem, locus of control, hippocampal volume, and cortisol regulation in young and old adulthood'. *NeuroImage*, 28(4), 815–26.
45. Ochsner, K. N., et al. (2002), 'Rethinking Feelings: An fMRI Study of the Cognitive Regulation of Emotion'. *Journal of Cognitive Neuroscience*, 14, 1215–29.
46. Duncko, R., et al. (2007), 'Acute exposure to stress improves performance in trace eyeblink conditioning and spatial learning tasks in healthy men'. *Learning & Memory*, 14(5), 329–35.

6: *Can Too Much Happiness Be Bad for You?*

1. Bianchi, E. C. (2014), 'Entering Adulthood in a Recession Tempers Later Narcissism'. *Psychological Science*, 25(7), 1429–1437.
2. Ibid.
3. Twenge, J. M., et al. (2010), 'Birth cohort increases in psychopathology among young Americans, 1938–2007: A cross-temporal meta-analysis of the MMPI'. *Clinical Psychology Review*, 30(2), 145–54.
4. Smith, V. and A. Ennos (2003), 'The effects of air flow and stem flexure on the mechanical and hydraulic properties of the stems of sunflowers Helianthus annuus L.', *Journal of Experimental Botany*, 54(383), 845–9.

5. Seery, M. D., E. A. Holman and R. C. Silver (2010), 'Whatever does not kill us: cumulative lifetime adversity, vulnerability, and resilience'. *Journal of Personality and Social Psychology*, 99(6), 1025.

6. Gunnar, M. R., et al. (2009), 'Moderate versus severe early life stress: associations with stress reactivity and regulation in 10–12-year-old children'. *Psychoneuroendocrinology*, 34(1), 62–75.

7. Seery, M. D., et al. (2013), 'An Upside to Adversity? Moderate Cumulative Lifetime Adversity Is Associated With Resilient Responses in the Face of Controlled Stressors'. *Psychological Science* 24(7), 1181–9.

8. Seery, M.D., et al. (2010), 'Lifetime exposure to adversity predicts functional impairment and healthcare utilization among individuals with chronic back pain'. *Pain*, 150(3), 507–15.

9. Robertson, I. H. (2013), 'A noradrenergic theory of cognitive reserve: implications for Alzheimer's disease'. *Neurobiology of Aging*, 34, 298–308.

10. Robertson, I. H. (2014), 'A right hemisphere role in cognitive reserve'. *Neurobiology of Aging*, 35(6), 1375–85.

11. Mor, N. and J. Winquist (2002), 'Self-focused attention and negative affect: a meta-analysis'. *Psychological Bulletin*, 128(4), 638.

12. Robertson, I. H. (2010), 'Anosognosia and Error Processing in Various Clinical Disorders', in G. P. Prigatano (ed.), *The Study of Anosognosia*. Oxford: Oxford University Press.

13. Harty, S., et al. (2014), 'Transcranial Direct Current Stimulation over Right Dorsolateral Prefrontal Cortex Enhances Error Awareness in Older Age'. *Journal of Neuroscience*, 34(10), 3646–52.

14. Singh-Curry, V. and M. Husain (2009), 'The functional role of the inferior parietal lobe in the dorsal and ventral stream dichotomy'. *Neuropsychologia*, 47, 1434–48.

15. Brickman, P., D. Coates and R. Janoff-Bulman (1978), 'Lottery winners and accident victims: Is happiness relative?', *Journal of Personality and Social Psychology*, 36(8), 917.

16. Collicutt McGrath, J. and P. A. Linley (2006), 'Post-traumatic growth in acquired brain injury: A preliminary small scale study'. *Brain Injury*, 20(7), 767–73.

17. Eisenberger, N. I. (2011), 'The neural basis of social pain: Findings and implications', in G. MacDonald and L. A. Jensen-Campbell (eds), *Social Pain: Neuropsychological and Health Implications of Loss and Exclusion*. New York: American Psychological Association, 53–78.

18. Kalisch, R., et al. (2005), 'Anxiety reduction through detachment: subjective, physiological, and neural effects'. *Journal of Cognitive Neuroscience*, 17(6), 874–83.

19. Collicutt McGrath and Linley, 'Post-traumatic growth in acquired brain injury'.

20. Kalisch et al., 'Anxiety reduction through detachment'.
21. Ochsner, K. N., J. A. Silvers and J. T. Buhle (2012), 'Functional imaging studies of emotion regulation: a synthetic review and evolving model of the cognitive control of emotion'. *Annals of the New York Academy of Sciences*, 1251, E1–E24.
22. Harmon-Jones, E., P. A. Gable and C. K. Peterson (2010), 'The role of asymmetric frontal cortical activity in emotion-related phenomena: A review and update'. *Biological Psychology*, 84(3), 451–62.
23. Mason, L., et al. (2014), 'Decision-making and trait impulsivity in bipolar disorder are associated with reduced prefrontal regulation of striatal reward valuation'. *Brain*, 137(8), 2346–55.
24. Anderson, G., 'Did cocaine use by bankers cause the global financial crisis?' 15 April 2013, *Guardian*.
25. Service, M. F., 'Fraudster Bernie Madoff "had so much cocaine in his office it was dubbed the North Pole". 21 October 2009, *Daily Mail*.
26. Mihov, K. M., M. Denzler and J. Förster (2010), 'Hemispheric specialization and creative thinking: A meta-analytic review of lateralization of creativity'. *Brain and Cognition*, 72(3), 442–8.
27. Goldstein, A., et al. (2010), 'Unilateral muscle contractions enhance creative thinking'. *Psychonomic Bulletin & Review*, 17(6), 895–9.
28. Chi, R. P. and A. W. Snyder (2011), 'Facilitate insight by non-invasive brain stimulation'. *PLOS ONE*, 6(2), e16655.
29. Rowling, J. (2008), 'The Fringe Benefits of Failure, and the Importance of Imagination', in *Harvard Gazette*. Cambridge, Mass.: Harvard University.

Epilogue

1. Dweck, C. S. and A. Master (2008), 'Self-theories motivate self-regulated learning', in D. H. Schunk and B. J. Zimmerman (eds), *Motivation and Self-regulated Learning: Theory, Research, and Applications*. New York: Taylor and Francis, pp. 31–51.
2. Blackwell, Lisa S., K. H. Trzesniewski and C. S. Dweck (2007), 'Implicit Theories of Intelligence Predict Achievement Across an Adolescent Transition: A Longitudinal Study and an Intervention'. *Child Development*, 78(1), 246–63.
3. Dweck, C. and E. Leggett (1988), 'A Social-Cognitive Approach to Motivation and Personality'. *Psychological Review*, 256–73.
4. Parent, M.C. and J. L. Alquist (2015), 'Born Fat: The Relations Between Weight Changeability Beliefs and Health Behaviors and Physical Health'. *Health Education & Behavior*, doi:10.1177/1090198115602266.

5. Molden, D. C. and C. S. Dweck (2006), 'Finding "meaning" in psychology: a lay theories approach to self-regulation, social perception, and social development'. *American Psychologist*, 61(3), 192.
6. Garber, J., M. K. Keiley and N. C. Martin (2002), 'Developmental trajectories of adolescents' depressive symptoms: predictors of change'. *Journal of Consulting and Clinical Psychology*, 70(1), 79–95.

Index

A NOTE ON THE AUTHOR

Ian Robertson is a clinical psychologist and neuroscientist with a unique ability to apply his research to the pressures of everyday life. His previous books, *Mind Sculpture*, *The Mind's Eye* and *The Winner Effect*, have been translated into many languages and he is widely recognised as one of the world's leading researchers in neuropsychology.

ianrobertson.org
@ihrobertson

The text of this book is set in Adobe Garamond. It is one of several versions of Garamond based on the designs of Claude Garamond. It is thought that Garamond based his font on Bembo, cut in 1495 by Francesco Griffo in collaboration with the Italian printer Aldus Manutius. Garamond types were first used in books printed in Paris around 1532. Many of the present-day versions of this type are based on the Typi Academiae of Jean Jannon, cut in Sedan in 1615.

Claude Garamond was born in Paris in 1480. He learned how to cut type from his father and by the age of fifteen he was able to fashion steel punches the size of a pica with great precision. At the age of sixty he was commissioned by King Francis I to design a Greek alphabet; for this he was given the honourable title of royal type-founder. He died in 1561.